THE NECTAR OF
IMMORTALITY

THE NECTAR OF
IMMORTALITY

SRI NISARGADATTA MAHARAJ'S
DISCOURSES ON THE ETERNAL

EDITED BY
ROBERT POWELL, PH.D.

BLUE DOVE PRESS
SAN DIEGO, CALIFORNIA • 2001

The mission of the Blue Dove Foundation is to deepen the spiritual life of all by making available works on the lives, messages, and examples of saints and sages of all religions and traditions as well as other spiritual titles that provide tools for inner growth. These books are distributed in our *Lights of Grace* catalog, our bookstore, and also on our website: www.bluedove.org. For a free catalog contact:

The Blue Dove Foundation
4204 Sorrento Valley Blvd. Suite K
San Diego, CA 92121
Phone: 800-691-1008 or 858-623-3330
E-mail: bdp@bluedove.org
www.bluedove.org

Second printing, 2001

First published in Great Britain 1987 under the title *The Nectar of the Lord's Feet*

Printed in Canada

Cover and text design: Brian Moucka
Cover photo courtesy of Jack and Diana Masson

ISBN: 1-884997-13-9

Library of Congress Cataloging in Publication data:
Nisargadatta, Maharaj, 1897-
The nectar of immortality : Sri Nisargadatta Maharaj's
discourses on the eternal /
edited by Robert Powell. --1st American ed.
          p.   cm.
   "First published in Great Britain 1987 under title:
The Nectar of the Lord's Feet"--CIP t.p. verso.
Includes bibliographical references.
ISBN 1-884997-13-9
1. Spiritual life--Hinduism. 2. Hinduism--Doctrines.
I. Powell. Robert, 1918-   . II. Title.
BL1214.26.N576   1996
294.5'22--dc20

                                95-44138
                                CIP

If one obtains and relishes the nectar of the Lord's feet, the *charan-amrita*, the mind can be conquered. This means that the mind will no longer hold sway over us; its mastery imposed on us from childhood will no longer oppress us...

But how can such a state be attained? Only if one totally accepts the knowledge "I am" as oneself with full conviction and faith and firmly believes in the dictum *I am that by which I know "I am."* This knowledge "I am" is the *charan-amrita*. Why is it called *amrita*—the nectar? Because... by drinking nectar, one becomes immortal. Thus, a true devotee, by abiding in the knowledge "I am" transcends the experience of death and attains immortality.

———◆◆———

Consciousness does not shine by itself. It shines by a light beyond it. Having seen the dreamlike quality of consciousness, look for the light in which it appears, which gives it being. There is the content of consciousness as well as the awareness of it

———◆◆———

To expound and propagate concepts is simple. But to drop all concepts is difficult and rare.

SRI NISARGADATTA MAHARAJ

ACKNOWLEDGEMENTS

This book has come about through the combined efforts of a small number of Sri Nisargadatta Maharaj's devotees, and to them the Editor expresses his gratitude.

My special thanks are due to Mr. Saumitra K. Mullarpattan, who not only was the chief interpreter during these conversations but also checked the transcripts for accuracy of the Marathi translation into English.

Thanks are also due to Dr. Lance Nelson of the University of San Diego, California, Dr. Jeffrey M. Masson and Dr. R. Ranganathan for invaluable assistance rendered in the compilation of the Glossary.

SRI NISARGADATTA MAHARAJ

Born in Bombay in 1897. His parents, who gave him the name Maruti, had a small farm at the village of Kandalgaon and it was here that he spent his early years. In 1924 he married, later becoming a cigarette trader in Bombay where he and his wife raised a family. From early childhood he had taken a keen interest in spiritual matters, his talks with holy men sharpening his inquisitive mind and kindling a spiritual fire. At the age of 34 he met his Guru and three years later realized himself, taking the name of Nisargadatta. He continued to live the life of an ordinary Indian working-man but his teachings, which he set out in his master-work *I Am That* and which are rooted in the ancient Upanishadic tradition, made a significant philosophical break from contemporary thought. Devotees travelled from all over the world to hear Nisargadatta's unique message until his death in 1981.

ROBERT POWELL

Born in Amsterdam in 1918. After obtaining his doctorate in chemistry he pursued a career as a science editor and writer, at first in Britain and later in America. Robert Powell's personal exploration of spirituality began in the 1960's, and his quest for self-discovery led him to study Zen and a number of spiritual masters including J. Krishnamurti. His own spiritual awakening coincided with his discovery of the teachings of Sri Nisargadatta. He has written a number of books on what he describes as "human consciousness transformation" and lives with his wife Gina in La Jolla, California.

CONTENTS

FOREWORD

Whenever "new" discourses arrive from an authentic sage, they become in the hands of enthusiasts one more "path", "way", "method", "discipline", "truth"—in short, the very latest means of self-liberation. No wonder gurus and yogas enjoy vogues; they come and go.

What distinguishes Sri Nisargadatta Maharaj is that "his" way, *atma-yoga*, is not offered as the best way among other ways. Rather, he recalls us to the essence of yoga itself. This requires the most absolute pause lest we try to go beyond where we have not yet begun. Just as the essence of a thing is not the manifest thing itself (e.g., the essence of yoga is not its manifest practice), so, analogously, Maharaj would not have welcomed being regarded as one distinguished being among other beings. This posture shocks our ordinary thinking in our ordinary way. Still, if instead of bolting at this seeming unintelligibility, we accept his invitation to press into the heart of things with our mind, but in "his" non-ordinary way, we shall with time enjoy a settled disposition for *atma-yoga*, the essential yoga of self-inquiry. And this he cheerfully calls us to undergo.

Now the essence of yoga is *to let* Reality be realized. Letting-be is not to do or to make anything. I cannot realize what Maharaj calls me to do if I begin by generating new concepts, remembering old ones or by manipulating myself or others. What then is left? These transcripts edited by Dr. Robert Powell are in themselves sufficient to make this question and its answer clear. This foreword is not an attempt to paraphrase them, but to suggest very briefly what might prove helpful perspectives in which to study them.

The ordinary life lived in the ordinary way is lived out within a conflict of motives. Vision and practice in one's personal career do not harmonize with one another. Authentic yoga enables them to coincide. From the standpoint of vision Maharaj offers a definition of self that is at once philosophically profound and spiritually exact: "I am that by which I know 'I am'." This situates the self at the source rather than at the estuary of concepts and language to realize which brings the mind to silence and release from self-misunderstanding.

From the standpoint of practice, the general province of yoga, the matter is much more refractory to language. This is because, as the sage says, "You accept a concept and stop at it. Thus your spiritual progress stagnates at the conceptual level." It is precisely this that sabotages meditation, namely, grasping at a concept. Therefore the counsel " . . . just be, do nothing . . . Nothing is to be done. Then all your riddles will be solved and dissolved." It is the supra-relational intuition of the primordial "I am" that authentic meditation discovers.

Finally, "where" is this intuition realized and held? At the borderline of beingness and non-beingness, precisely where the intellect "subsides." Here, Maharaj introduces us to the field of authentic yoga and reveals his genuine spiritual warriorhood. Let us pause momentarily at this borderline even if only conceptually. On the one hand the sage says "World is experiential but 'You,' the Absolute, are non-experiential." On the other hand, "This 'you-are' experience has come as a fever. How and why this fever has come, for this there is no explanation or reason."

Given his doctrine in the round, Maharaj does not leave this phenomenon quite so summarily. He cannot do so if he means to assert factually a "borderline of beingness and non-beingness" which he calls the *maha-yoga* (cf. *Bhagavad Gita* 2:16). This borderline, the intersection between the Absolute and the phenomenal, is "where" Reality is discovered. True, in the absolute sense there is no way to know why this fever "you-are" has come, any more than one can know why there should be something and not, rather, nothing. But it is not true relatively, since without the possibility of illusion there is no condition for enlightenment. "The refusal to see the snake in the rope is the necessary condition for seeing the rope" (i.e., the rope as rope). This statement from Maharaj's *I Am That* clarifies the status of the "borderline" and in effect affirms the snake's or *maya*'s role in self-awakening. How beautifully his teaching avoids the presumption of a direct assault upon Reality, as though Reality is an experience, and avoids also the mindless self-identification with phenomena.

Letting oneself become stabilized at the "borderline" entails courage and perseverance. The sage declares in *I Am That*: "I do not need convictions, I live on courage. Courage is my essence, which is love of life. I am free of memories and anticipations, unconcerned with what I am and what I am not. I am not addicted to self-descriptions, *soham* and *brahmasmi* ('I am He', 'I am the Supreme'); these are of no use to me, I have the courage to be as nothing and to see the world as it is: nothing. It sounds simple, but just try it!"

These conversations point to that luminous depth which lies beyond thought and speech, but words are required to say so. Accordingly, it is in unborn and undying gratitude that we thank Sri Nisargadatta Maharaj, Dr Robert Powell and all those whose special knowledge and devotion have made the transmission of these last transcripts available for our continuing meditation.

Allan W. Anderson
Professor Emeritus
Religious Studies Department
San Diego State University
San Diego, California

PREFACE

The message which comes through loud and clear from Sri Nisargadatta Maharaj's final teaching is: Return to what you were before your so-called "birth"—the emergence of a particular body with which you have identified yourself so willingly and unthinkingly. Be in that eternity, which is a state of wholeness, even though your body may be broken; a state of riches, even though you may have no earthly possessions; a state of imperturbable peace and quietude, even though the world around you may go up in flames.

That state before birth is even now, and ever now—because it is before time itself, before time in the guise of "becoming" emerged as the tyrannical concept that rules our life and enslaves us. It is the changeless reality from which all change has sprung—space, time, the entire world of experience, and all our cherished illusions. Thus, to ponder over and take to one's heart Maharaj's wisdom is truly partaking of the nectar of the Gods, because it restores us to our original pristine and blissful condition, the rediscovery of our Source.

INTRODUCTION

What these discourses are really about is Transcendence—"going beyond"—and Sri Nisargadatta Maharaj is a true Master at the Art of Transcendence. Without perceiving the actual nature of this transcendence, one can never properly understand Maharaj because all one's efforts remain a mere intellectual activity. And one of the great pitfalls in the spiritual quest is to get stuck on a particular level, all the while thinking one has attained the final goal.

The process of transcendence in this case consists of two phases. First, by thorough understanding of what one *is* operationally—through "care-full" observation and contemplation—one may come to a realization of the sense of being, or the consciousness of "I-am-ness," in its pure state—without the slightest taint of "individuality." For this consciousness is actually the universal consciousness and is realized only through transcendence of the "me."

Essential in this realization is the understanding of one's real identity, which has been obscured by our identification with the body. The body itself is inert and does not proclaim any identity. By identifying with the body we are imposing limits on our Self, where in reality there is none. Thus, we are the totality in which all objects and "personalities" appear and disappear but in itself is "personality-less" or impersonal. Upon cutting this false identification with the body, our real nature manifests as formless—bodiless and mindless—in which the mind is viewed as mere "internal noise," or an artificial (i.e. conceptual) framework superimposed on a state of No-Mind, the manifest dynamic consciousness. In this state one has no needs and demands, and so there can no longer exist any problems.

It should also be seen clearly that this consciousness or beingness—the sentience which distinguishes us from a lifeless lump of flesh—has come upon us like a stranger in the night, beyond any apparent causality. Although in itself of a strictly temporal nature and intermittent in its manifestation, it ever strives to maintain continuity in time through anchoring itself to the sense of body and the memory of the manifold experiences and conceptual images that make up the body's mental associations.

The second phase of the process of transcendence is that in which even this beingness or universal consciousness is transcended. The beingness, in its aspect of knowingness, transcends itself, leading to the realization that one is that beingness as phenomenon or manifestation only, but fundamentally one is not that at all. One is none of these temporal things because space-time has no reality outside our being; it has come about with the beingness as a mode of perceptual experiencing—that is, as an experiential framework which enables us to observe the essentially formless and timeless as "objects" in sequential manner. So what is one then, when all the superficial and superimposed appearances have been removed? One is what always has been and always will be, timelessly, the Source, or the Absolute, which has spawned this entire relative world. On the other hand, because the beingness is strictly temporal, it cannot even support itself. It needs the support of the Absolute, and so ultimately we are That.

One common problem is that we wish to *reach* That, when in reality we *are* It all the time. We think that self-realization consists in "becoming aware of," "know," "experience," or "understand" the Absolute—all modes of duality that apply only to the beingness. Does a fish in the ocean, in order to function, have to have a certain awareness of water? Do human beings, while living in space, need special understanding of space?

Maharaj, in this connection, states paradoxically: "Whatever you understand, you are not. In non-understanding you understand yourself." Best, therefore, simply to *be*, without trying to think (on it)—that is, without superimposing distraction as "mind."

What pains us particularly in this is the complete reversal of accepted social values. To view our ultimate Reality as a kind of Nothingness or Emptiness, an eternal Stillness rather than continuous movement and activity towards some useful end is like standing things on their head. The point is that we live essentially for the waking state. In this state we do things as a "doer," working towards our imagined security and happiness, and in the process gather ever more "experiences." At the same time, the sleep state is considered an irrelevant interval, if not a "waste of time," and a fearful reminder of Death. But the truth is the very opposite: the waking state only is "time," and all that is part of the beingness which is inevitably to be lost. So what, ultimately, is the use? The concept that things have an ultimate usefulness—which, on the most profound level is the same as Time in the Absolute—must be dropped as erroneous; as Maharaj stated so pointedly: "Even the Highest is useless to the Highest."

In dreamless sleep, all the memories of the day's activities are lost and there is then no problem at all; there is no "time" (to pass or waste), and when we wake up we have only the memory of a blissful state. The fact of the matter is that the waking state is only another dream and part of the same mechanism that causes us to dream in our sleep.

The twofold transcendence as sketched above may perhaps be further clarified by the following analogy. While looking at a motion picture, we are so taken by the apparent reality of the moving figures on the screen that we momentarily forget they are actually the shadows cast from a large number of static pictures, and that what we are really looking at is the screen only. In this observation, the screen is the only reality; all else is appearance and therefore illusory. This analogy relates, respectively, to the separate individualities in our world perception and the universal consciousness or beingness. Yet, ultimately, this screen would not have been observed but for the light from the projector—which is what we actually perceive as reflected by the screen. Similarly, the beingness could not have manifested without the light of the Absolute. And just as the physical light itself cannot be perceived directly but only through reflection against a surface, so the Absolute (as pure subjectivity) cannot be experienced directly but manifests, as consciousness, only through its reflection against the relative world (as "object"-ivity).

Maharaj on many occasions introduces a little Hindu cosmogony when referring to whatever happens in the beingness as the action of the "three *gunas*"[1] on the "five elements"[2] and their interplay. One reason is obviously to establish a connection with these classical Hindu notions that are so familiar to the Indian portion of his audience. However, I suspect that a more important consideration is to stress the strictly impersonal nature of the world process which absolutely does not allow for the presence of a "doer." After all, if we have come about as the result of such interplay of impersonal elements, we are essentially still that only ("impersonal") since at no time has an individual entity been introduced except as concept. At other times, Maharaj refers to the universal consciousness as the "chemical," emphasizing its inherent mechanistic character.

Thus, we are ineluctably led to the conclusion that everything happens by itself, and that an individual doer is totally a figment of our imagination. One could also say that a separate "I" would have entailed the infusion or "creation" of an

---

[1] and [2] See footnotes on p. 11.

individual soul on a fundamental level. Having understood
what our real nature is, it now appears that Maharaj has
miraculously transcended all theories of "Creationism"!

It should further be noted that Maharaj throughout his
teachings explicitly or implicitly transcends all other duali-
ties as well—even the basic question whether duality or
non-duality is the nature of the ultimate reality, long a bone
of contention in Indian philosophical thinking. On the level
of beingness or manifestation, through seeing that all divisions are unreal and that not a thing has self-nature or an
intrinsic identity, one comes to the clear conviction that the
ultimate reality is Non-Duality or *advaita*. However, even
this understanding becomes invalid when transcending the
beingness itself on the level of the Absolute or Unmanifest.
The Absolute, being attributeless or non-qualitative, cannot
be said to be even non-dual; it lies beyond both duality and
non-duality.

Another way to approach this problem would be to ask:
"Who poses this question about duality or non-duality?" He
must himself be of the nature of duality or non-duality, as the
case may be, and this renders his conclusion in the matter
meaningless. Because, as Protagoras has phrased it so elo-
quently, "Man is the measure of all things," the world perception is necessarily contiguous with the nature of the
perceiver. This means that the answer is already contained in
the question and so really only defines the limits of the ques-
tioner. Meditation on this point silences the questioning
intellect and leads to its transcendence.

The duality of theism and atheism is likewise transcended. God or gods can only be in the realm of beingness. In
Maharaj's scheme of things, God is not of the Highest, for
even God needs the support of the Absolute. As he so often
stated: "For God to exist, you must be there first. Without
you, God cannot exist."

Finally, Maharaj transcends the separate paths of *bhakti*
and *jnana*—Devotion and Knowledge. Both approaches can

lead to the Highest. It depends on one's disposition and aptitude which serves him best, but the ultimate flowering in the moment of grace is identical—the final surrender of the ego. It is an event that transcends any path and any personal attributes. Thus Maharaj's uniqueness is perhaps the universality of his teaching, which is equally valid and pertinent to the heart-oriented and the head-oriented person, the East and the West.

THE NECTAR OF
IMMORTALITY

EDITOR'S NOTES:

The basic truth of what the great *advaita* masters teach is essentially the same, which is to be expected since there is only one Reality. However, different teachers lay different emphasis on various aspects of this teaching and to this purpose employ slightly different nomenclatures or use these terms in flexible ways as it suits their purposes.

Thus, **I-am-ness** and **beingness** in these conversations are generally used by Maharaj as denoting limited states of understanding which are fundamentally based on a sense of separate identity, resulting from taking oneself to be the body. They are wholly conceptual. Often, Maharaj uses both terms interchangeably. At other times, depending upon the emphasis he wishes to convey, he denotes beingness as a somewhat superior state, which arises upon transcendence of the "I-am-ness" and equates the manifest consciousness. Maharaj also refers to beingness as **consciousness** or **knowingness** and according to him it still is the product of the five elements (rooted in materiality). Thus, he states: "This knowledge 'I am' or the 'beingness' is a cloak of illusion over the Absolute. Therefore, when Brahman is transcended only the *Parabrahman* is, in which there is not even a trace of the knowledge 'I am'." The state[1] of "beingness" is clearly an incomplete, provisional state of understanding, as is also evinced from Maharaj's following words: "The sages and prophets recognized the sense of 'being' initially. Then they meditated and abided in it and finally transcended it, resulting in their ultimate realization."

Whereas "I-am-ness," "beingness" or "knowingness" has a somatic basis, which in turn arises from the physical elements, the Absolute lies beyond all "physicality" and can no longer be described. In the Absolute one has no instrument to make any statements. What I am in the absolute sense, it is not possible to convey in any words. In that ultimate awareness, nobody has any consciousness of being present. The presence itself is not there in the Absolute.

Maharaj teaches that upon transcendence of the individual consciousness into the universal manifest consciousness, the latter rests upon and lies within the Unmanifest or *Parabrahman*, where the latter

---

[1] The term "state" implies a "condition," a modification, of a more basic reality, which concerns an unalterable and ineffable substrate. Therefore, it would be more accurate to express this modification as a superimposition on the "non-state" of the *Parabrahman*, somewhat analogous to the seeing of a snake in the rope.

denotes "that principle which was unaffected by the dissolution of the universes" and is a non-state. He also declares: "Please apprehend this clearly that You, the Absolute—bereft of any body identity—are complete, perfect and the Unborn." In his teaching, you—as the Absolute—never have or had any birth. All forms are a result of the five-elemental play.

This *Parabrahman* lies beyond both duality and non-duality, since it is prior to space and time (we can only properly talk of duality or non-duality within the physical-mental sphere, i.e. within consciousness.) It is the Absolute or the Ultimate Subject, what one *is*, for there is no longer anyone or anything—not even the consciousness—to experience it.

Finally, it must be noted here that other sages as well as classic Vedanta scriptures are commonly using "I-am-ness" and Beingness (spelled with a capital B) interchangeably with the *Parabrahman* or Absolute, and the Absolute is then referred to as Consciousness (with a capital C) and consistently denoted by the term "Self" (Sri Ramana Maharshi) and as the "I-Principle" (Sri Atmananda).

Even this consciousness is not everything and it is not going to last for all time. Find out how that consciousness has arisen, the source of the consciousness... What is this body? The body is only an accumulation of food and water. Therefore, you are something separate from either the body or the consciousness.

Sri Nisargadatta Maharaj

Jivatman is the one who identifies with the body-mind as an individual separate from the world. The *atman* is only beingness, or the consciousness, which is the world. The Ultimate principle which knows this beingness cannot be named at all. It cannot be approached or conditioned by any words. That is the Ultimate state.

Sri Nisargadatta Maharaj

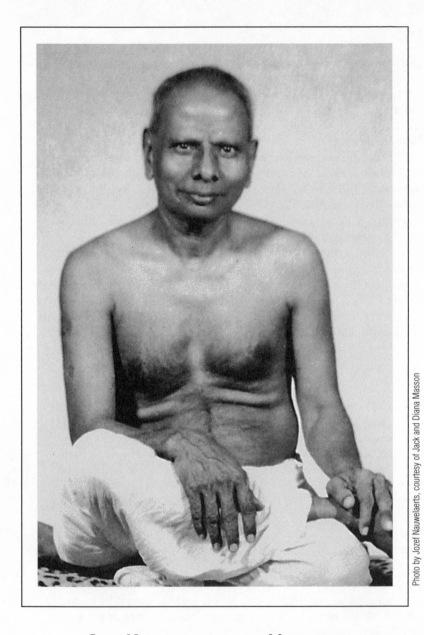

SRI NISARGADATTA MAHARAJ
1897 – 1981

1.

PRIOR TO CONCEPTION, WHAT WAS I?

 ISITOR: After self-realization, does a man still have ego?

MAHARAJ: He has no acquaintance whatsoever with the ego. So long as one identifies with form, the ego is there. Since a self-realized one no longer has any identification with the body form, the question simply does not arise. And what's more: of his very existence he is not even aware.[1] That means the self-realized principle witnesses the manifest principle, which is the life force together with the beingness.

V: When one has no form, a person has no more problems?

M: Not a line of the body touches him. That self-realized entity witnesses all the manifest, together with the world and also beingness.

V: In the case of one who has self-realized, do all body actions happen spontaneously?

---

1 According to Maharaj, all existence, which implies limitation, is unreal. Thus, a *jnani* is not aware of his existence as a limited entity, for he is awareness itself. For further elucidation of this point, see e.g. *I Am That*, p.355, first American edition.

2 · *The Nectar of Immortality*

M: All actions happen spontaneously. When the beingness was conceived, the body formation took place spontaneously around it; there was no question of building the body by someone.

V: In the case of a *jnani*,[2] one who is established in the Absolute, how can things happen around him for his sustenance? With a child, nature has provided parents so he can develop with their help, but the *jnani* has nobody around him.

M: When the beingness was in the womb, formation of the body occurred spontaneously, did it not? Similarly in the case of a *jnani* since he is one with nature, he is nature itself, so it is the worry of nature to look after him; no personalities as such are required, everything just happens around him.

V: There are all these great yogis who try to live for thousands of years. They hang upside down, live on air or just on water. What is it that interests them, and why are they living so long with so much suffering?

M: They get some kind of satisfaction out of it, the fact that they are doing something spiritual, are doing penance. They want to prolong that and feel they have a certain duty by prolonging their life in the spiritual field. On what does this beingness depend? Because of what do you survive? This life does not continue. Why? When something goes wrong with the body, it comes to an end. You are confident that you are, but what does it depend on? And through what cause does this confidence, this beingness, disappear? In the process the beingness becomes "non-being." And "non-being" in turn becomes spontaneously being. Now whom should we question as to how this happens?

2 A self-realized Master (literally: "knower").

One has to investigate oneself. You have the faith "you are"; on what does it depend? Nobody investigates on these lines. Why this beingness, how am I, why am I, on what does it depend? This aspect is never considered; people consider only the relative factors concerning the body-mind, and the area beyond that they never look into.

What do you mean by "death," a common word, a common parlance? This faith "I am" has disappeared, the confidence that "I am" is gone—that is death.

V: Some people want to prolong their life; it means that they have self-love. Does it mean that they are within the limits of *maya* (illusion), or have they transcended it?

M: Once you have transcended the body idea, it does not matter whether you live a short or a long time. You do not depend on anything for your existence. Try to find out for yourself what you are, without depending on anything or anyone.

Whatever you want to think or ponder over, it is something other than the "you" you think of. You ever ponder over something which you are not! Then, how to think about yourself? This you cannot do. Perceiving this clearly, you become thought-free. Whatever you do, you think about something which is not you, even with a noble thought like Ishwara (God), which is still conceptual and therefore apart from yourself. Now, is it possible to think of one's own Self, that is the question?

V: You say that we should be independent of our functional being (i.e., the existence of body-mind), which I try to do, but somehow I cannot be independent of my health.

M: You should ask questions about the subject we are dealing with. You ask gross and irrelevant questions. I am dealing with a topic where one has to ponder on oneself; there is no

scope for words (concepts). Also, when there are no words
there are no thoughts.

What were you doing, eight days before conception in the
womb of your mother, do you know or do I? Explain to me
the situation prior to entering the womb, how were you? Only
you can say anything about that state.

V: I do not remember, but. . . I was beingness?

*Translator: Beingness comes in the womb. Beingness in a dormant
condition, in the fetus in the mother's womb.*

M: Who knows about the beingness before conception? If
you had been aware of the beingness before conception, you
would not have cared to enter the womb.

V: I do not remember.

M: It is not possible because it is a nonattentive state. So,
where is the question of remembering? With beingness,
attention starts later. Beingness comes in the womb in a dormant condition. That borderline between being and "non-
being" is *moolamaya*. Glorious names are given to it. Initially,
there is no attention, and suddenly attention begins.

Here is an article [*Maharaj shows his cigarette lighter*]; before it
came into existence, what was its name? From "non-being" into
the being state, how was it observed? You just felt that touch.
Before observing anything, we feel the touch of "I am."

To realize that state prior to conception, that eternal
state, whatever that state is, to abide in that is the highest.
Now, for your sake, I attach a name to it, the *Parabrahman*
state—the Absolute.

V: Before conception?

M: Before conception, whatever state exists, that is your most natural perfect state, it always prevails. When this beingness goes, that state will still be there, it ever prevails.

The state in which you were eight days prior to conception and millions of years back, whatever it was, that state prevails and now also it does, and after the departure of the beingness it still prevails!

Because of my present state of health, I am not inclined to talk much. Dealing only with this topic, only a rare person will understand what I am driving at. When someone asks me some gross questions, do you expect me to come down to that level and explain all details as if in a kindergarten class?

I have some very strange questions! Before my birth, at my conception, who pulled me into the womb? My father? My mother? And in what form? That would be a possibility provided I had a certain form, color or design prior to conception; then only could I have been pulled inside. The one who has solved this riddle comes to the conclusion that this beingness and this entire manifest world is unreal.

There is no need for knowledge when this beingness was not. When even great gods like Brahma and Vishnu were confronted with this puzzle, they closed their eyes and went into *samadhi* and just disappeared.

V: They did nothing?

M: What could they do? At present you feel "you are" because of the association with the vital breath; because the vital breath is operating, you know "you are." When the association is not there, what can you do? Can you actually do anything?

V: What can I do to acquire knowledge?

M: Do nothing except hold on to yourself, just be in that beingness, then it will tell you how beingness turns into "non-beingness." Therefore, I tell you just one thing: Catch hold of that touch of "I-am-ness" only, that beingness, dwell on it, and contemplate on that only.

V: The best thing to do is to be there in that "I am" state? To be is meditation?

M: There is no "be there," just *be*.

V: Is it possible the whole day? Any special meditation?

M: Who says for the whole day? Who else can say for the whole day except the beingness? It can capture everything in this contemplation, but it cannot capture itself.

V: Is *karma* a problem which we create?

M: The one which has created you has created this *karma* and the problems of *karma*, so that you involve yourself in it. Who has created you? What do you mean by *karma*? It is movement, activity.

V: As long as one is subject to *karma*, one encounters it and it appears as something real. But is it not actually an illusion?

M: I try to keep you trapped as though you were in the womb. If you listen to me carefully and quietly, everything will be sprouting. It is a common mistake, a blunder, that we have become identified with the body form.

V: The last mistake?

M: The first and the last. Again remember the words which I have spoken earlier. The seed which has created this body and everything else, so long as it is alive, moist, you will explain these words. Once that seed is gone, you are in eternity only, in your eternal state.

Out of a very small seed a very big tree grows into the sky. Similarly this small seed, this beingness—"I-am-ness" touch—out of that seed all this manifest world is created. At this point there is no energy left in the words; therefore, you cannot further express it verbally.

V: My ego, my body, the other bodies of the egos here in this room, what they are hearing are all concepts, movements in this beingness. Is this correct?

M: Yes, if you want to understand more clearly, take the example of a dream, your dream. Since I am touching on the highest aspects of knowledge, I am not in a position to reply to any gross questions. If somebody talks, or asks questions, I am not going to challenge him, because to him, from his standpoint and from his level, those are correct questions. Right now, if I have to be interested in a state at all, it is that state eight days prior to conception, the *Parabrahman* state. Yesterday the word "ego" was used, as also today. On what level is this "ego" attached, and when?

Everything is most sacred and most unsacred. The question of sacred and unsacred is there so long as that beingness is there. If the beingness is not, where is the question of sacredness or non-sacredness?

You meet some persons and call them very knowledgeable. They will tell you that in the next birth you will be a great king and in the birth after that a still greater king. When such advice is given, the listener is very happy, very contented. Self-love is the underlying illusion, but nobody wants to admit that. Nobody wants to give up his beingness, his "I am" knowledge.

Suppose the following question is directed to an intelligent person: "Prior to conception, how were you?" This person would reply as follows: "I was in a dormant condition in the essences of my parents." That would be how a smart person would reply. It is, however, based on the conventional

outlook and if you trace it further to the parents' parents,
etc., you will have an infinite regression on your hands.
Therefore, this principle, which has no form but is only the
knowledge in a dormant condition, if you trace it to its source
it goes back to eternity. That is why the principle is eternal.
Now I will give you two clues for further investigation. One is
to establish yourself in that state prior to conception, and the
other is that you wrap yourself up in the traditional concept
of the parents. In the latter case, you will fail to get a good
grip on the true nature of yourself. The conventional knowledge is not destroyed but there is no need for it, because
basically it is unreal, it is untruth. Whatever an ignorant child
or an accomplished sage says, both are correct.

I can give you another concept: "Who is the perfect principle or the personality that existed prior to the birth of anybody?" Here again is a similarity between a child in the cradle
and a perfect *jnani*. When the child tastes food, he does not
know whether it is urine or fecal material, food or milk, all
these things having the same taste for him.

How does the child know himself in that state? Only *he*
knows. Now what do you want to say about the child and the
jnani?

V: I believe it is important to become a child, to drop all the
attachments.

M: Where is the question of giving up, renouncing everything? It has come about spontaneously, you do not have to
throw out anything. You have to understand only. You are
compelled to suffer or experience only because of the appearance of the beingness. Did you go and catch hold of the
beingness? It has come about spontaneously. Is the child
catching hold of something, has he caught any concepts,
ideas or an ego? A *jnani* having understood this state of
beingness and all its play, has transcended it and abides in
the state prior to conception. He dwells ever in that perfect

state, whether the beingness appears or disappears.

During your life you have accomplished so many things, you had so many identities and all these identities and that understanding have left you. Finally, with what identity will you die?

If you have understood what "you" really are, is there any necessity for spiritual pursuits?

V: In reality, no. I ask myself why I am here, what is the reason? I know only too well there is ignorance in me. I think the reason I came here is to get help to destroy that ignorance.

M: Your ignorance is gone. Now, describe, what do you mean by ignorance?

V: I do not perceive it clearly enough, although I see many things. Sometimes I have problems; I think it is because of my ignorance.

M: The waking state, sleep, beingness, all this experience combined, is ignorance only. That ignorance termed as "birth" means these three. Once you know this, you can do anything, you are free. When you know the false as false, then you do not have to worship at all. Any idea of doership—that things happen because you do something—also goes away.

Prior to the appearance of this beingness, you were purely *Parabrahman*, the Absolute.

The *jnani* does not give importance to this waking, sleeping and beingness. Just as you are not afraid of a serpent made out of rubber, so in a similar way the *jnani* has no interest in this waking state and beingness.

V: Is it all the same?

M: Will you make use of this knowledge? To see and affirm it as false, need you make any effort?

V: You can see anything without effort.

M: Once you know the ignorance, then there is no effort, because you have dismissed it as ignorance and there is no registration of it for future reference.

What are you suffering or experiencing? The name of this body form and its associations and that beingness. If you ponder over it, you will have the instant solution.

V: You have talked about the state of conception. Also that we are in the eternal *Parabrahman* state; but what is *karma*, is it a variant of that eternal state?

M: There is no *karma* in the state of *Parabrahman*. Where is the question of *karma*?

V: But you were talking about conception, body-mind.

M: Who has entered the body-mind form?

V: I...? We...?

M: Now the space has entered in this room, the space is there. Why and how has the space entered this room?

V: At first there was no space...no time?

M: The space is outside, the space is here also; there is no distinction between outside and inside space, it is all space only! So where is the question of coming and going?

January 8th 1980

2.

THE EMERGENCE OF BEINGNESS

ISITOR: I feel that Christianity leads from body-mind to consciousness but does not go beyond it.

MAHARAJ: Regarding Christ, Krishna or any other prophet, please understand one point clearly. When they became embodied, the raw material and equipment which went into the process were the five elements only.[1] Further, the beingness which emerged out of those embodied forms was an outcome of the interactions of these five elements. It expressed itself through the three *gunas*[2] and lasted only so long as the five-elemental food essence was available. And when the beingness disappeared, these saviours did not know their existence nor their performance in their embodied state.

When and how does one first have the experience of the world? This experience becomes possible only after the emergence of the beingness out of the five-elemental food-essence body. Now this beingness is something like a telescope. An observer views the sun, moon, stars etc. through the telescope. But the observer is neither the telescope nor its field

---

1 In Hindu philosophy the "five elements"—earth, water, fire, air and ether—are considered the fundamental building blocks of the entire physical universe.

2 The three *gunas*—*sattva* (purity, clarity, harmony), *rajas* (passion, energy, activity) and *tamas* (inertia, resistance, darkness)—are the basic attributes or qualities that underlie and operate the world process, according to Hindu teachings.

of observation. Similarly, witnessing of the five-elemental manifest world and cosmos happens to the Absolute, that is, to the Unborn eternal principle called the *Parabrahman*. But the Absolute—the Witness—is not the beingness, the medium of witnessing, and is also not the manifest universe witnessed.

Now a question. Ten days prior to your conception, what were you doing?

V: Only observing.

M: This reply is incorrect. From what standpoint do you talk? I want to nail you down to the point of the telescope. I bring you down to the beingness, but you digress. About which telescope did I talk to you? Right now, which is that telescope? It is made up of something; it has emerged out of something. Instead of concentrating on this point, you are babbling about this and that, and consider yourself knowledgeable. Is it not a telescope, through which you experience and observe the world? But you, the Absolute, are not the telescope. Are you?

Better stay put here at this point, in the beingness. But you jump here and there, leaving your standpoint. Then how will you get peace?

V: That is the whole name and game of life.

M: With your present attitude, no amount of knowledge will bring you peace. The beingness is given innumerable names and titles. It took nine months to create this telescope—this beingness—out of the five elements. Do you ever ponder over this? With that telescope, all this is experienced and seen, but the Observer is not the telescope.

V: In Lord Krishna's statement, there was never a time when I was not ...

M: Through the telescope, that is the beingness, which is the expression of the Observer only, he witnesses the manifest world. But do you think that the Observer has also disappeared when the telescope and field of observation are gone?

To say that an object exists, there should be two conditions. One is the object, and the other is the observer of the object, who says "the object is." The primary quality of the beingness is the sense of "I-am-ness." Later, there arises a multiplicity of qualities. But the Observer—the Absolute—is totally free from any qualities; therefore, it is called *nirguna*, which means "non-qualitative," "attributeless" etc.

V: You agreed that Krishna could not make any statement, when he was not in the body form, because there was no one to make it.

M: Certainly, because Krishna, in the Absolute state, has no instrument with which to make a statement...and to whom!?

Once you realize that all these goings-on are the products and play of the five elements, in the realm of the beingness, you remain unaffected by it and apart from it.

My attention is only on the medium by which I know "I am," and by which I experience the world. I pay no attention to the *siddhi* powers and anything that appears. The only relevant question is, how did this medium happen to be?

Visitors come here with acquired knowledge and they expect me to comment on it. How can I? They are already clogged up with that knowledge. So let them fend for themselves.

A dead man does not interfere with the affairs of a live one. Similarly, the one who has understood and realized the beingness is not interested in the activities and happenings within the domain of beingness.

Here we are discussing knowledge that transcends the beingness. But, in the world, who is really interested in such profound knowledge?

It is a great privilege that you are inclined to listen to such talks. Many people would not care for the talks, in spite of the opportunities.

V: There is a story of a Zen Master. When a disciple visited him, the Master shouted, "Why have you come? Are you not dead yet?" Also Ramana Maharshi had said that the mind should be totally killed.

M: Throw out all your talking, concepts and words! After all, what is the mind? It is just the noise that goes on inside.

With waking begins the chattering, and the talk goes on endlessly thereafter. This is your mind, and you run after it. Your breath itself is the talk. If the breath stops, there can be no talk.

V: As I reflect on the matter, I find that love and truth are the same, and I also understand that realization of love is quite beyond the mind.

M: All this talk is at the mind-level. But I do not talk from the standpoint of the individual, but from the level of total manifestation. An individual understands himself through certain concepts and accordingly undergoes pleasure and pain. But in actuality this is not so. The mind, which interprets happiness and unhappiness, is meant for conducting affairs in the world.

V: The rituals of worship—such as waving of lights, that is, *arati* and singing of *bhajans*—are necessary to keep alive our fervor for God and to prevent drabness.

M: What is the meaning of *arati* as you understand it?

V: Special love.

M: In the Marathi language *arati* means "special need." This special need is the love that every animal has for itself. It is that love to *be* that prompts each animal to carry on activities in the world; it is the inborn nature of all the species. Because of the identification of each species with its own kind, the idea of "otherness" springs up and it is this "otherness" which is the root cause of pleasure and pain. Love to *be* is the self-love. Who does not love himself? This very love is called *atma-prem* or "Self-Love."

Because a human being considers himself an individual, he suffers pain and pleasure; only in the state of consciousness there is no such question of happiness or unhappiness—these are experienced only at the body-mind level. I have transcended this state of body-mind—that is, the individual state—and am talking to you from the dynamic manifest consciousness. The very concept that "good" or "bad" is going to happen is completely wiped out from me. Also, I do not have any concepts regarding birth and death.

My physical condition is so weak. Any other person in such a state would not even be able to get up.

Total loss of pride in individuality is my *nirvana*; that is, the state of non-identity. You carry out all your worldly and spiritual activities with an identity. So long as your individuality is not lost, you will be bothered by pleasure and pain, past and future, birth and death, etc.

Have you ever thought along these lines? Who asks you this question? I, the formless, the dynamic, manifest consciousness, am asking you.

Why do you suffer pain? You have compressed yourself into a form and an identity, hence the suffering. You pursue spirituality from the same limited and conditioned standpoint and hence you cannot secure any foothold in these pursuits. In whatever subject you are absorbed, you deal with it from the standpoint of a personalized entity, and not as dynamic manifest consciousness. The knowledge that "you are" is manifest and all-pervading. It is purer and subtler than this light and therefore it cognizes light. Since you hold on to the individualistic memory, you are unable to digest this knowledge and so you have no peace.

There are any number of *hatha-yogins*, as well as persons who recite holy names (doing *japa*) and those who practice austerities (*tapa*). Ostensibly, many of them are on the spiritual path. But they rest content with the acquisition of *siddhi*-powers for indulging in miracles. They cannot make progress towards real spiritual knowledge, and they pride themselves on their particular systems, the powers acquired and their individualities. This is not spiritual knowledge at all. A person in service should either be satisfied with his meager salary or quit his job. Similarly, a *jnani* should be satisfied with the three states of waking, deep sleep and knowingness or quit them. I as a *jnani* am telling you my story. What is the use of this alternation of deep sleep and waking to me? I do not want it. This perceptible universe is limitless and infinite. By preserving it what shall I gain?

Since a realized sage abides in perfection, he has no need at all to gain anything. However, a seeker will obtain million-fold benefits by merely remembering and dwelling upon the life of the sage, so great is its potential. An ordinary person cannot even get a glimpse or inkling of the Absolute state of a *jnani*. He has to be satisfied with the behavior and physical expression of the *jnani*, evidenced as an outcome of his beingness. Such a sage, however, is neither the bodily expression nor the beingness. For example, a military officer wears a uniform with appurtenances which denote his rank. All this makes up the officer, but the uniform and the appurtenances are not the officer. Thus your body, which is a food-packet, is not you, but the indwelling principle of "you-are-ness" in the body is that "you" in essence.

You are not able to give up your identity with the body. This is the great *maya*—the Illusion. Therefore, you do not imbibe what I say.

V: How does a *jnani* know that he is realized?

M: When he recognizes his knowingness, which is the sense of "I am." Right here and now, you are in the realized state. But you try to judge it through desires and mind-concepts, hence your inability to apperceive it and abide in it.

In the *jnani* state, there is no need for anything, not even to know oneself. You are attached to the body-senses. There-fore, even though you may attain an age of hundred years, you still would crave for more years.

V: Sir, do you not feel sorry and concerned for us ignorant seekers who visit you?

M: Why should I? I am the very sun of knowledge and look upon everybody as such.

V: What is the significance of astrology, stars, good luck and bad luck?

M: Everything is important at the appropriate place. The one who has not recognized his true identity will naturally be after the "significance" of astrology, stars, luck, and so on. But for the one stabilized in the Self, nothing is important and significant. Such a one is not concerned with anything.

V: The Absolute state is said to be eternal. How is it that out of such a state of eternity, an ephemeral and temporary state like beingness should arise?

M: For the appearance of such a temporary state there must be a cause. For example, there are two intimate friends, who are in harmony with each other, but suddenly they start a quarrel. There must be some cause for this: some friction, some misunderstanding. Similarly, there must have been some cause to give rise to the five elements and the manifest universe out of the Absolute state. This primary cause is beyond explanation.

Just as the friends were separated by their differences and friction, the primary elements—space, air, fire, water and earth—were formed out of the Highest, as a result of friction and interaction. As the process continued, a variety of forms were created leading to the vegetable and animal kingdoms.

In the vegetable kingdom, termed *vanaspati*, we find shrubs, plants, trees etc. which grow in one place and do not move about. The next stage of evolution is termed *vachaspati*, the animal kingdom, which abounds in germs, worms, animals and human beings. These species have the privilege of movement and communication.

Human beings, though biologically animals, are a superior species and are termed *brihaspati*. Because of the highly evolved indwelling principle, which is consciousness, a human being is able to acquire wisdom intuitively and transcend itself into the Highest. During the process his consciousness, initially conditioned to the body-mind, develops into the universal consciousness, amply justifying the title *brihaspati*. This means "Lord of the immense magnitude," connoting the all-pervading principle. Ultimately, the universal consciousness subsides into the Absolute.

V: Is there any physical pain when the vital breath leaves the body?

M: One who is involved with concepts suffers at the time of death. The intensity of suffering is in accordance with the meaning of concepts held on to. One who is devoted to God and free from concepts dies happily and peacefully as though going into a slumber. Do you suffer when you fall into sleep?

The poet-sage Tukaram mentioned in one of his poems that vegetation is our kith and kin, and it is also our ancestor. But how could it be otherwise when vegetable essence is an absolute necessity for the creation of the animal kingdom, the *vachaspati* family, and also the *brihaspati* family of the human species?

The Gods in the heaven have to take a human form, to manifest on the earth, and their bodies have to be sustained and nourished on the vegetable essence. To reach the godly state, one must have a human body and consciousness.

To abide in the highest state you have to do nothing else but listen to these talks carefully and then everything will happen correctly, conducive to your spiritual progress.

Now I have told you about the beingness, which is the outcome of the five-elemental play and the result of the food-essence body. But "You" as the Absolute are not the body, and not even the indwelling beingness. Then why should you worry about its departure?

V: Since we are born, we are going to die ...

M: A *jnani* is not born and he does not die. But when the body of a *jnani* drops off, people around him may weep in sorrow, because they identify with their bodies. They therefore consider a *jnani* to be an embodied person, which, however, he is not.

V: How is it that a *jnani*, abiding in the "non-knowing" state, is able to communicate with us?

M: A *jnani* is so called, because he is in possession of *jnana*— the beingness—which is sustained by a body. While in possession of *jnana*, a *jnani* is in the "non-knowing," Absolute state. The beingness and the body are the media of communication for a *jnani*. But he is not the language expressed for communication.

You too, could be in the *jnani*-state provided you recede and abide in a state prior to emanation of words in you. Such a state is revealed at the borderline of deep sleep and the waking state, which is the very beginning of emergence of the consciousness.

This state is known as the *para-shakti* or *para-vani* state, which is the source of words or language. From this source, which is the first stage, until it finally explodes out of the mouth for communication, the language has to pass through three more stages—that is, four stages in all. The second is *pashyanti*, the incipient stage, where the intangible formation of language begins. The third stage is *madhyama* or the middle stage, in which the tangible formation of language takes place in the zone of the mind. The fourth and last stage is *vaikhari*, when the breath causes the language to explode from the mouth into vocal expression.

Para-vani is the subtlest form of language. This term has a deeper connotation. *Para* means "the other," indicating separateness from the Absolute state, but the closest to it.

A *jnani* or Lord Krishna says, "I am not the *para-vani*," because they abide in the Highest. When I talk about Krishna, do not take him to be a personality; he is the Absolute.

One feels one has "understood" when some concept, title or name like "Krishna" is given; but that is not the way. One has to *be* Krishna to understand him truly.

Para-vani is not the language of the Absolute, as it is still an outcome of the beingness. After passing through various stages of development, it finally expresses vocally a concept, which on our acceptance possesses us. In the process we identify totally with the concept and lose our true identity.

V: Once in my meditation, I stabilized in the *para-vani* state, prior to mind, and saw visions of the past and future.

M: In the *para-vani* state one gets *siddhi*-powers and can read the past and future. It also leads to the awakening of the *kundalini* energy.

January 9th 1980

3.

TIME IS THE CHILD OF A BARREN WOMAN

ISITOR: What is the difference between physical suffering and psychological suffering?

MAHARAJ: When there is disorder in the body, suffering is physical; but when there is disturbance due to thoughts and concepts, the suffering is psychological. Have you any idea when all this began?

V: I do not know.

M: It is spontaneous and it is inside. But how and when was registration made of the first day of life?

V: From death, birth took place; prior to that there was no consciousness.

M: To what was this title of birth given? Just look into that, what is really born?

V: A concept is born.

M: Even to say that a concept is born, is not the full truth. What did actually happen?

V: Time and space appeared.

M: You will have to do plenty of *dhyana-yoga* to come up with a correct reply. There are any number of *Upanishads* and yogas like *hatha-yoga*, Patanjali yoga, and others. But I know only *atma-yoga*, which is Self-knowledge and nothing else.

Out of a common heap of wheat, many types of edibles are prepared, using different methods. In the same way, there are many systems of spirituality. I am not interested in nibbling at the various delicacies—methods and techniques—but only in the main course, which is the primordial Source of all existence.

How and why did the state of my beingness, my existence, and the entire manifestation arise and out of what? In that original source, there is no feeling of my presence. To that ultimate source, how did the state of existence resulting in differentiation (duality) happen?

The Upanishads and various systems of yoga are conceptual fantasies. I did not go into all these at all. I inquired only about my "non-beingness" and beingness, and how and why they did come about.

V: That I am born is itself . . .

M: But this is a concept which you have accepted. It is a hearsay.

V: Every moment we are born.

M: Yes, every moment births take place. But what is that material which is born?

V: Whatever that maybe?

M: On the "non-beingness" beingness has appeared; and in the beingness, thousands of births and live forms are created within a moment.

V: But the background of all this is "nothingness" only.

M: There should also be a knower of this "nothingness," and this knower is "nothingness," too! In the "non-beingness," how could that be expressed and who would? In that state, there is no subject and no object, and it is called *nirvishaya*. But in the beingness state, both subject and object are there, hence it is called *savishaya*.

Have you understood that Pantanjali yoga deals with duality? Have you studied the yoga? Does it deal with yoking[1] or unyoking?

V: I have read a little. The yoga deals with duality.

M: Out of what did Patanjali create duality? When he established duality, what did he divide? Whatever he divided, was it not in the realm of beingness—in the sphere of subject-object?

V: The moment one tries to divide something, it becomes "objective."

M: But the ultimate principle is prior to the sphere of subject-object. I would like to know how you divide that state.

On the state of "non-beingness," the beingness appeared together with manifestation, creating a feeling as if "I am." Who that is, is not important; only "I am" is important.

We talked about duality. Did it begin with the appearance of beingness over "non-beingness" or has it developed later? It is simple. When the beingness—that is, the "I-am-ness"— is felt, it is obvious that Quality.[2] has begun. Later, the being-ness manifests as multiplicity, functioning as it does through

---

1 The term 'yoga' stems from the Sanskrit *yuga*, meaning yoke or union.
2 That is, awareness of attributes, qualities, has become possible in the consciousness.

innumerable forms. The initial humming of the beingness as "I am, I am" is the duality. But who accepts the duality? The "non-beingness" accepts duality with the beingness. The Absolute "non-being" state, by assuming the being state, becomes dual in manifestation.

Words create duality between us. Two persons are sitting quietly and so there is no quarrel. But the moment they start talking, duality begins.

When the "non-being" state expresses objectivity[3] through the being state, the latter is called *maya*, the female aspect, while the "non-being" state is considered the male aspect. Therefore, the functioning of the manifest universe is called the play of *prakriti* and *purusha*—that is, the female and male aspects.

V: I was trying to follow a path through which this beingness could experience the "non-beingness," which amounts to the manifest experiencing the Unmanifest. Right from the start we must understand its impossibility.

M: I have been telling you the same thing. You should do plenty of deep meditation. The beingness should totally merge in the "non-being" state. Every day I get rid of my stress and strain when going into deep sleep. In this way, I forget myself, undergoing oblivion and relaxation. Thus, the beingness should be lost in the "non-beingness."

When the *dhyana-yoga* is done correctly, the beingness dissolves gradually into "non-beingness." In the intermediate state between deep sleep and waking, a dream vista presents itself. Similarly, in deep meditation, all the necessary wisdom is revealed to you. After understanding all this and realizing that the manifest world is unreal, do you still consider yourself a personality? The beingness state is the manifest state. It is not individualistic; it is made up of the five elements, three

---

3 The world as "objects"; that is, the manifest.

gunas, and *prakriti-purush*—the female and male principle. The beingness later merges into "non-beingness."

That is why I say my process is *atma-yoga*, which means abidance in the Self. When the "non-being" state became the being state, the world, along with so many things, came into existence. As per my guru's directive, I became one with the beingness. Beingness means having the vision that one is the entire dynamic universe. When one transcends individuality, one is the manifest beingness only. In this process the Unmanifest reveals itself.

V: This is what Maharaj calls meditation; that is, to remain in the state of beingness.

M: There is no creator and nobody created me.

V: The creator is already the manifest. First we need the sense of being before we become the creator.

M: The creation takes place through his mind and concepts. Through the humming in his mind, his world is created. Even if you are alone, your mental blabbering and chattering go on.

V: Also, the mind is created.

M: Yes, but when? When the "non-being" turns into being, then only the mind appears and functions. Only a very rare person, one in a million, will take the correct delivery of my talks.

V: Once the delivery is taken, there is no "person."

M: There is no question of "yours" or "mine." In the ocean of my manifestation, millions like you are crawling around, like waves and ripples.

V: With the exception of a guru, all others are ripples.

M: But what is a guru? Is he a material sustained on a piece of bread?

V: It is another word for the indescribable. My guru told me that first I as an individual should accept a guru, and that the guru would lead me initially to the manifest and then to the Unmanifest.

M: But the guru is the manifest state. If you accept individuality you will not make progress. You must identify with the manifest totality from the first moment of daybreak. The light of complete clarity is flooding all round. In this way you identify with the manifest as a whole, you are all-pervading. On the other hand, if you hold on to an individual entity, you cannot progress. Since death is inevitable, why should I not abide by the directive of my guru? By following him implicitly, effortlessly and spontaneously, the manifest becomes the unmanifest, beingness merges in the "non-beingness." Unmanifest means total quietude and rest; then there is no birth and death, no coming and going.

Worldly activities are not possible without the humming of beingness. Individuality and manifestation are the outcome of the "non-being" state turning into beingness, like the waking of a person from deep slumber. A person in deep sleep and the person fully awake are one and the same. The one who sleeps is also the one who wakes up.

V: The waking state is another word for the world.

M: Waking means total world manifestation.

V: When he is awakened, he always goes back to dualism.

M: Because I talk to you, you continue to talk to me. If you know any earnest person, bring him also here.

V: Very rarely I tell somebody to come here; once or twice, I have done so.

M: I like people who are eager to understand. I throw out anybody who likes only to argue for the sake of arguing.

I ever abide in the Unmanifest. But everything happens due to the power of *yogamaya*, the beingness, which is also the manifest state.

A great Marathi poet refers to the Unmanifest state in his poems, and brings out the following. "Just think of a barren woman, untouched by anyone, who conceives and delivers a child." In the same manner, the *yogamaya* has delivered the manifest world. That is, the beingness, which is the outcome of the food-essence body, has projected this manifestation, and it is the image of my guru. The Unmanifest and the manifest, the *yogamaya*, can never be together.

V: A person translated the book *I Am That* into a foreign language, and he wants to give it the title of *Tat-Tvam-Asi*.

M: I do not like that. Either keep the title *I Am That* or none at all.

V: But Mr. Maurice Frydman had agreed.

M: I do not agree. And also do not dilute the contents of the book with your understanding, even though you may consider yourself a *jnani*. Do it the same way Frydman did; the exact and original text should be translated, with no modifications.

V: I now realize after meditation that the essence of your teachings is contained in *I Am That*.

M: If you want to realize the meaning of "I Am That," go into deep meditation, but "you," the manifest, should merge in "You," the Unmanifest. That is the ultimate meaning. Whatever experience I get of the world and God, is not due to any favor or obligation of God but is entirely due to me, because of my state. If I were not, I would not have had the experience. I did prevail and do prevail always. Because of my beingness I experience the world. I now see clearly the oneness in the teachings of three seers or *acharyas*—Shankara, Madhava, and Ramanuja.

All the creations emanate from the *moolamaya*, the primary illusion and its secret humming. All words, talks and titles refer to those emanations. Similarly, all these images are the chatterings and expressions of somebody. The images are the products of the love-talk and coming together of two persons.

The state of beingness is termed as God. The godly state is the entire manifestation. It is my state in experiencing; it is duality. But my Unmanifest state is non-dual, and in that state there is no experiencing and manifestation. I, the Absolute, am not the state of being.

In spite of all the spiritual knowledge, you are not inclined to give up the experiences at the body-mind level. If you do not identify with the body-mind sense, you will transcend into the beingness first, and later, you will transcend even the beingness. However, you want to keep your individuality at the body-mind level as well as experience and be in both the beingness and "non-beingness states, which is impossible.

I, the Absolute, am the witness of my beingness, which is the total manifestation. This state is being glorified with very high attributes, such as God, Maheshwar etc. and worshipped by many people. To them, such a talk of mine may smack of mischief.

V: If I say "I am not That," then there is also "I am That."

M: Experience does not mean the experiencer.

V: The experiencer is experienced. The experiencer is an object, but is taken for a subject. I experience you and "I am" is an object, but is treated as a subject. Is it an illusion to see an object as subject?

M: If you say you talk, you are a liar. All this talk of yours is intellectual, only in reply to my talk. Do you directly practice what you talk?

V: It is practice. I have been looking everywhere for an "I." Wherever I go in search of "me," I am not there.

M: "I" is not the word "I," it is everything.

V: "I" as an individual am not able to get to that everything.

M: I do not accuse anyone of being a personality. You identify yourself as an individual. Fear of death does not allow you to transcend into beingness.

V: Only the false wants to continue as the false.

M: "I," the Absolute, am not the personal "I." The personal "I" cannot tolerate the impersonal beingness and is afraid of death.

The factual, eternal "I," the Absolute, has no fear of death.

That which you want to sustain, nourish and maintain by five-elemental stuff, is not you. Since you identify with something unreal, there is the fear of death.

"You," the Absolute, are not the personal "you." But for all the twenty-four hours, the personal entity "you" is watched, nourished and protected so that it may continue on and on. In short, you watch, nourish, protect and guard that which you are not in actuality.

V: When you meet a lion, you have two alternatives. Either you run away or you allow yourself to be eaten by it.

M: There is a third alternative. You threaten the lion since either way it is going to kill you. So why die like a coward out of fear? Attack it bravely and knock out some of its teeth.

One who is afraid of time becomes a prey of time. But time itself becomes a prey of that one who is not afraid of it.

One who transcends time, the beingness and its attributes, abides in the Absolute.

A *jnani* consumes time continuously, while all others are being devoured by it. A *jnani* is beyond time, (the five) elements, attributes and emotions.

V: We have to be very careful that we do not set up something as real that one intends to consume.

M: You presume to be a *jnani* but you are filled up with so much stuff. To fear time is like fearing an unborn child.

V: I did not state that I consider myself to be a *jnani*.

M: Time is the child of a barren woman. [*Maharaj is pointing to the visitor and another person.*] Both of you are eminent personalities known for spirituality and you have come well armed to attack me. But I tell you, you cannot locate me.

Why am I not afraid of time? Because even the dissolution of this manifest universe, the Brahman, cannot destroy me. Prior to, during and after the dissolution, I, the Absolute, ever prevail, untouched, untainted and unchanged.

While dying, with what identity will you die? If you are certain of your death, why suffer a lowly death? Die nobly and honorably. Before death, be the Highest, be the Infinite, the Absolute.

January 14th 1980

4.

Nothing Ever Interferes with the Five-Elemental Play

ISITOR: What is ego? Why does it think about itself all the time?

MAHARAJ: First you have what is called *aham-bhava*—that is, the "I-am" sense. Later, this sense identifies with the form of a body, when it is called *aham-akar*, the "I am" form. This is ego.

V: Why does it not disappear in people? They feel they are the doers and they want to be loved.

M: It is the natural outcome of the three *gunas*. While the body is the product of food essence, it is the medium through which all these three *gunas* function. Ego is the very nature of these *gunas*. While a man thinks that he is the doer, even though he does no action, in reality all activities are due to the *gunas*; only a *jnani* realizes this and transcends the ego. Ego is never a title or a name, but just a sense of "I am" prior to words. The waking state, the sleep state and the knowingness "I am" constitute an ego. In the absence of these three states, what do you think you are? What would be the evidence for your existence?

V: Could the ego not be due to thoughts?

M: These three states are the natural outcome of the being-ness or "I-am-ness." One who recognizes beingness tran-scends all the three *gunas*, namely *sattva*—consciousness; *rajas*—dynamic quality; and *tamas*—claiming doership. But for the manifestation of consciousness a food body is absolutely necessary. Without such a body, there cannot be consciousness, the three *gunas*, nor even the three states—waking, sleep and knowingness.

V: Do your refer to consciousness as "mental" consciousness?

M: Where does the mind come in, when we talk about the three states? Without waking, deep sleep and knowingness, where is the mind? You do not know "you are" without con-sciousness.

V: Could it be then that thoughts appear in consciousness?

M: [*Pointing to the burning incense stick*] Yes, when the incense stick burns, the fragrance will be there. What do you mean by birth? It means: birth of the waking state, deep sleep and knowingness. But the material for this birth is the quin-tessence of the food body. If you have any questions, by all means ask. But who will take care of your questions, if you are not? If you are not, where can be your questions, even those relating to your birth and death?

V: Birth happens only to the body.

M: But when you refer to the body, is it not the quintessence of the food essence?

V: What causes the ego to expand sometimes with age, and with the deterioration of the body, as in paranoids?

Ego seems to increase with age.

M: But of what is ego the product? Whatever experience you undergo, it is the product of beingness, and beingness is the outcome of food. From food is derived the body form and from the body essence is derived the birth. What else do you want? With the appearance of beingness, the title of birth is given to you; that is, you are accused of having been born.

With such replies, your questions and talk lose all significance. Now tell me who is talking? Are you doing the talking or is it the quality of beingness that is talking?

V: There never is an "I" that is talking.

M: You still do not grasp what I say. The seed of world-experience is the beingness. Where is the "I" in all this? The talking is done by the beingness. But it is dependent upon the body essence, which is the product of food. When the food essence in the body loses its quality, beingness becomes weak and death is feared. [*A visitor mumbles something inaudible.*] Use any words you like, but express yourself; you have written books, but what information did you give in them? "I am" or "I am not" relates to the beingness. All the words are spoken by the beingness. If the sense "I am" is not, which means if the beingness is not, who is there to say "I am"?

V: I never had the idea that I was writing a book.

M: What is the use of discussing with you? There is no point in your denying what I said. What are you, and what could you be without the three states, waking, deep sleep and the knowingness "I am"?

V: Therefore I deny that I am doing anything.

M: But there appears to be some assertiveness in your talking. Please do not try to talk merely for the sake of talking. If you would quietly listen, everything will be revealed. When anybody comes here, I know that the person does not have an iota of knowledge. People bring me presents. But this is a disease, and "I" am not into that. Similarly, in our life, physical and spiritual disciplines and rituals are prescribed, but I am ever out of these conditionings. This is absolutely clear to me.

This Chinese carpet, said to be worth more than four thousand rupees, has been presented to me. But I have no feelings about it at all. Similarly, I am not the least concerned with the so-called "birth" imposed on me. The birth relates to the three *gunas*, the three states and the beingness, and I am not all that.

I use the carpet, but I am not the carpet. In the same way I use the beingness. Persons visiting this place fall at my feet out of respect; but the respect is shown to the quality of beingness, and I am unapproachable.

All this spiritual knowledge pertains to the realm of beingness, and it is bound to go like a guest. The question is, where, when and how will you have the ultimate knowledge?

V: Who has this ultimate knowledge?

M: Nobody has the self-knowledge. The knowledge "I am" is not the Absolute state.

The beingness, comprising the three *gunas*, is given the godly titles of Brahma, Vishnu and Mahesh. Brahma is the creator, Vishnu is the preserver, and Mahesh is the destroyer, and the combination of these three gods is worshipped and praised by us when singing *bhajans*. But all these gods subside and go to rest in a self-realized sage, termed as *jnani*. The state of a *jnani* transcends the sense of time and even the sublime emotions. That highest state is given the title of *Parabrahman*, *Paramatman* etc.

After reading spiritual books, people argue over their

interpretation. But what is the point of such quarrels? All these talks go on in the realm of beingness, and You, the Ultimate, are not the beingness.

V: Yesterday, Maharaj asked me to meditate on when the beingness appeared. Questions could also be asked about the state after the appearance of beingness—such as why, when, how, and so forth.

M: Yes, these questions can only be asked after the beingness appears, and the beingness will remain so long as the food essence is available. Why and when does a person die? When the food essence is not supplied, function of the person's body ceases and the indwelling beingness disappears. This is called "death." But who did die?

V: One object died.

M: But who says this? Can it be the one who died? If not, who says it?

V: You can see it from day to day, that this beingness appears and disappears. Something else must be there.

M: The ultimate seer cannot see by seeing; but without seeing, the seer sees. But that ultimate seer does not belong to the realm of the beingness.

V: It appears to me that seeing itself is seen.

M: But what is the cause of this? It is the beingness only—the three-aspected *sattva-guna*. If you do not understand, please keep quiet.
   The Absolute cannot be understood.
   Whatever you understand, you are not that. In non-understanding, you understand yourself.

V: Then how can the three *gunas* be responsible for the witnessing?

M: [*Addressing a new visitor, with a beard*] You have grown and maintained a beard like a Mahatma. Come on, ask questions.

V: You talked about a *jnani*. Does he think? Can he be without feelings?

M: For the purpose of communicating, he has to employ such words as "the *jnani* is thinking" or "the *jnani* is talking" etc.

V: But actually nothing of the sort is there. It is reassuring that he talks about thinking and that he is feeling.

M: The *jnani* is beyond the attributes of the three *gunas* and is beyond emotions. How can a *jnani* be involved in thinking and emotions?

V: I see a difference between thinking and emotions. By feelings, I mean those which are like the stream of a river; they come and go.

M: Yes, this appearance and disappearance of the feelings and emotions is the very nature of the three *gunas*, and not yours.

V: I understand this is a natural outflow of the *gunas* and nothing of the Absolute.

M: You are convinced about nothingness, but of whom? Are you convinced that a *jnani* is Nothing or the knowledge "I am" is nothing? The knowledge "I am" is nothing. That knowledge is like a guest; it comes and goes. You have come here; you are very clever. Now what did happen? All the knowledge, which you had collected elsewhere and brought here, is rendered useless and redundant. [*Pointing to two visitors*] The knowledge of these two will become useless. At present, they are the very ocean of knowledge. But when their three *gunas* and beingness disappear, all their knowledge also disappears. So long as beingness is there, all the worldly activities will go on. But you now realize that "You" are neither the activities in the beingness nor the beingness. "You," as the Absolute, are none of these.

V: To meditate on that which comes after the beingness . . . The only way I see it, is to watch what remains, when everything is gone. When time, space and everything disappear, what remains?

M: When the manifest world of the three *gunas* is gone, whatever remains indicates what you were a hundred years ago and prior to your birth. In that state, "You" were bereft of the three states of waking, deep sleep and knowingness. You should abide in that state during meditation.

V: How does one avoid going into *samadhi* in this meditation?

M: Going into *samadhi* or coming out of *samadhi* are not your qualities. You are beyond qualities.

V: My question is how to avoid it.

M: Going into, and coming out of, a *samadhi* are qualities like all other qualities of the three *gunas*. And do not try to avoid *samadhi*. It is the natural play of the three *gunas*. *Samadhi* will be there but "You," the Absolute, are not in the *samadhi*.

V: I used to have these tendencies, so my guru forbade me meditation and observation.

M: But could you tell me, how and where "You" were introduced to the knowledge "you are"? Did your guru tell you that? Where and how did the union of the beingness and the Absolute take place?

V: The question never did arise.

M: One ignorant person can tell another ignorant person anything. But that one who recognizes what the ignorance is, should be considered as the knower, the *jnani*. Many people presume themselves to be *jnanis*, but they are ignorant only. One person says "I am knowledgeable," another says "I know," but both are ignorant.

The waking state is followed by deep sleep, and deep sleep is followed by the waking state, and so on goes the cycle. This cycle constitutes the beingness.

You must be very alert, as at a time when someone aims a rifle at you and you are trying to avoid the bullet. It is not child's play to see through the ignorance.

V: I will try.

M: Are you going to ask questions from without the three states or within the three states?

V: By using the three states.

M: Then, what's the use? Earlier you wanted to stay here for three weeks. Do you still want to stay for that period? Is it necessary?

V: Earlier Maharaj asked me a question and I answered. But once my purpose is achieved I may go.

M: Is there anything left that you have not accomplished? And what do you mean by "purpose"?

V: May I know how to deal with the purpose completely and consciously?

M: The process of attaining the purpose is within the three *gunas*, whereas the purpose itself is beyond the three *gunas*.

V: The process of attaining the purpose then disappears?

M: The meditator involved in that process is not the real one, but the target is the real.

V: [*Pointing to a book*] This is the final obstacle.

SECOND VISITOR: What is the value of a book?

M: A book is valuable to its reader provided he is more ignorant than its author. The author has very beautifully written ignorance in his book, and we are so engrossed in it that we go to sleep.

V: But after reading that book many have come to you.

M: Why have they come?

V: It was to get direction for their meditation.

M: With the transcendence of the knowledge "I am," the Absolute prevails. The state is called *Parabrahman*, while the knowledge "I am" is termed Brahman. This knowledge "I am" or the beingness is illusion only. Therefore, when Brahman is transcended only the *Parabrahman* is, in which there is not even a trace of the knowledge "I am."

When those three states—waking, deep sleep and knowingness—were not there, could there be beingness? Why? In that state did your beingness arise? Would there be any necessity for beingness in the *Parabrahman* state? In the absence of beingness, did "You" see the sun, the moon and the stars in the firmament? In that state, was there any benefit from the sun, the moon and the stars?

The beingness is a superimposition, a cloak of illusion over the Absolute. In other words, the beingness, which is the very first and primary concept "I am," is itself the conceptual illusion.

This manifest world is the dynamic play of the five elements. In that there is no scope for an individual. A diamond radiates light all around; it is radiance itself. In deeper meditation, you will realize that, like the brilliance emanating from a diamond in all directions, the manifest world emanates out of you; it is your effulgence only.

V: Like an old-fashioned cafe having mirrors on the walls, which reflect your manifold images.

M: The whole universe manifests in that principle, which is termed beingness or birth. This beingness illumines all that exists, which means the entire universe manifests as the body of the beingness.

On a television screen, you see different forms, images and landscapes, but they are all the expression or play of the tube's electron beams only. Similarly, the entire manifest world of your purview is the product of your beingness.

When you go into deep quietude, after thorough comprehension of these talks, you will observe that in the knowledge "you are" innumerable universes and cosmoses latently exist. [*Maharaj pointing to the foreigners*] These are seekers of the true knowledge, while the local people follow devotion to a god, so that their mundane needs are provided. I have therefore the highest regard for the foreigners, because whatever they undertake they see it through to the very end. I admire their perseverance.

V: To come here, many of us have left all the profound *acharyas* completely.

M: Such spiritual personages do not belong to any country. They are the product of the five-elemental play. People take birth and die in the play of the consciousness. In the next hundred years all these people will die and a fresh crop of visitors will arrive in the world, in a continuous process. This too is the play of the five elements. Many *acharyas* have come and gone, but none could bring about even a little change in the process of creation, preservation and destruction—the play of the five elements. Not only *acharyas*, even great incarnations like Rama, Krishna and others, could not do it. The same can be said of the *rishis*, sages, and *siddhapurushas*—the souls highly evolved spiritually.

Inexorably the great drama goes on, although it is governed by such an odious principle as: "One species preys upon another species."

There are organizations to prevent cruelty to animals, but they only prolong the life and sufferings of animals. Could they bring to a stop animal creation? As a result of this creation, both the human beings and animals suffer in this world. Is there any progress in "family-planning" either in human beings or in animals in totality?

What authority does one have about oneself? People have no authority whatsoever to interfere in this grand drama of the five elements, to effect any change, because their primary nature ever remains the same.

January 15th 1980

5.

BEYOND THE *UPANISHADS*

MAHARAJ: I am not concerned with the miracles happening outside, but only with those happening within me.

In my original non-knowing state I did not know the sense of my being. But all of a sudden the beingness was felt spontaneously; this is the first miracle. Then in a flash I observed this enormous manifest world and also my body. Later, I conceived that the entire universe has manifested in the speck of my beingness only.

Why not pay attention to these miracles? A lot of miracles happen, each greater than the other. But what about these ones, I repeat. First, there was no message "I am" and also there was no world. Instantly, the message "I am" and this magnificent world materialized out of "nothingness"! How amazing!

This message "I am" is nothing other than the advertisement of the Eternal Truth. Similarly, the names, titles and forms of sages, seers and Mahatmas are merely announcements of the same principles. For example, when you prepare a number of dishes out of wheat, various names are given to them, but it is the wheat that is the basis for all the dishes.

To stabilize me in this Eternal Principle, my guru initiated me by pronouncing the sacred words *tat tvam asi*, which means "I Am That." From that moment onwards, I lost all interest in worldly affairs.

These sacred words are called the *maha-vakya*, which is a profound statement charged with sublime meanings.

VISITOR: What does "I am That" mean?

M: The word "That" in the statement refers to everything that is in the totality.

V: Can one get an inkling of the eternal state from any experiences obtained through the body and the world?

M: Certainly not. It is a non-experiential state. Prior to experiencing, what was my state? Who was there to reply to this? This is to be understood.

In that primordial state, I had no information about myself. Now a form, together with the information "I am," is impressed on me. You want to be told about this state and you want a name for it. If so, call it by the names *Parabrahman* or *Paramatman*. But to whom is the name given? To that "Me," who did not have a form and the self-information "I am."

You think you are wise and a *jnani*, and take pride in it. But do you ever think, how and why you are in this experiential state?

Just ponder on this. A lifeless puny ant was lying on the ground, almost invisible. While I looked at it, it showed signs of life and all of a sudden, a formidable lion emerged out of it! How can I take such a lion as real? On similar reckoning, how can I take the world as real?

All this creation and that which is called God are worshipped, but since when? That God emanated from the fluid energy and assumed a form. Though it is honored and revered, it is the product of spit. Is it not?

Prior to my assuming a body form, I had no information

as to who or from when or where I was. But the moment my guru aroused me with a call, everything was revealed.

This beingness of mine—the experiential state—is mean, low and despicable. The tiny ant referred to earlier was nearly dead. It had a fluid form, as a result of emission. Out of its wetness and fluid energy sprang the lion. This fluid was nothing but something like spit.

Out of the same fluid energy, a body form assumed a shape and it turned out to be a dwelling-place for the beingness; that is the state of "love to *be*." For that matter, whatever is created has the wetness of self-love, the "love to *be*," as its basis. The very wetness is also capable of manifesting itself into the entire movable and immovable world. In the body dwells the fluid energy and in the fluid energy dwells a latent body. This fluid energy is ethereal, subtle and most potent.

If you have any questions on this topic, please ask.

V: How can I go beyond the state of witnessing?

M: Your question is irrelevant. What did I tell you? Out of the spit, the "self-love" has taken a form. In the space of "self-love" manifests the entire universe, which is throbbing and pulsating with the same principle.

I have expounded this subject fully and you ask a question not pertinent to it. I have been explaining to you as to what "you are," and you have jumped to witnessing!

Did you comprehend that this source of beingness is the spit and that it is despicable?

V: Yes.

M: Do you know that your beingness is unreal, unworthy, lowly and a cheat? This beingness which prompts you to think "I am like this and I am like that" is illusory and fraudulent.

V: When one is a witness, it does not mean that one is like this or that.

M: At present you are not a witness. The question is, what is your present condition, what are you?

You want to show off by saying that you are a witness.

How was I in the absence of the message "I am"—that is, prior to beingness? I provided you with name tags for that state. These titles are *Parabrahman, Paramatman* etc.; they are only pointers to the state, but not the state itself. In the ultimate, they are redundant, extraneous and bogus.

V: Beingness is the witness and I know there is something beyond. Therefore, I asked a question: How to go beyond?

M: I am discussing about the beingness and its source, so also about the source of the body and the world, while you are talking about the world and its witnessing from the state of beingness.

The subject matter of the talk is that people believe in miracles. What I am saying is that there is no greater miracle than "I" experiencing the world. The primary miracle is that I experience "I am" and the world. Prior to this experiencing, I abided in myself, in my eternal Absolute state. The titles, mentioned earlier, refer to this state.

V: I have understood, but a little more explanation would be welcome.

M: Still more explanations! Then, am I not justified in saying that your head is full of sawdust? [*Maharaj asks a devotee to explain the matter again to the visitor, and not to digress from the subject.*] After meeting my guru, I gave up running after various sages and other gurus and directed my attention wholly upon myself.

Only if my beingness is there, can the existence of sages

and gurus arise. They last and flourish in my beingness, so long as it is there. Without my beingness—that is, without the message "I am"—my eternal Absolute only prevails.

V: That is precisely what I wanted to ask, when I said beyond the witness.

M: I am precisely telling you about my state. I am not giving you any other information. Probably you want to acquire knowledge for display and become a pseudo-guru.

Arising out of the beingness, its play and its subsidence are the three states of my beingness (waking, deep sleep and knowingness). When I talk with reference to "me," you should apply it to your own being and fully understand it, since all I said is identically relevant to you also.

Now these immature boys come here for spirituality. What can I say to them? If they insist on obtaining knowledge from me, I shall have to direct them to my sweeper, who can impart elements of knowledge when they do some service here like sweeping and cleaning.

In the hierarchy of our gods, there are some demigods who are to be appeased with the offerings of flesh and wine. Such lower deities received their spiritual powers after serving the higher deities as menial servants. Now suppose, one of such deities is angered and wants to wreak vengeance on me. What can she do? At the most, she will crush me under her toes and wipe out this emblem of the three *gunas*, which is my beingness. But who cares? Because, I, the Absolute, ever remain untouched. [*To the visitor*] Have you come here to have knowledge or learn how to become a guru?

V: I am not crazy.

M: Then why did you refer to "witnessing"?

V: Prior to coming here I was led up to the point of witnessing.

M: Witnessing what?

V: Everything that appears and disappears.

M: For the purpose of witnessing, that fluid—the being-ness—must be there.

V: Yes.

M: Then where is the question of witnessing? And witnessing what?

I have indicated to you how the incarnations and births continue to emanate out of the spit—the fluid energy. Apart from that, what are you?

V: Nothing.

M: Therefore, how can I judge anyone as good or bad? I reserve my judgement only for the source of all—the being-ness.

My approach is simple and straightforward. Out of the Absolute non-being state, the beingness together with the manifest world emerged before me. How did this happen? My guru revealed to me, while I was in deep meditation, how and due to what causes the manifest world of forms was created.

V: What was revealed to you in your meditation, and whatever your guru told you, are they very important indeed?

M: No doubt both are very important. But the eternal Absolute state of mine prior to the beingness, when the message "I am" was not, is supremely significant. Who would have witnessed the message "I am," if my priormost state of the "non-beingness" was not?

V: Who would have created them?[1]

M: The creation is self-effulgent and spontaneous. There is no creator. A magnificent tree sprouts out of a tiny seed. [*Maharaj asks the visitors to ask questions but none of them does, so he comments:*] Since I have put my axe at the very root of creation, how can any questions arise?

In the Marathi language, the word *moola* denotes the root of a tree; and with a slight modification in pronunciation, it means "child." Just as a splendid tree takes root out of a small seed, a full-grown person is latently rooted in a child and his beingness.

But I, as the Absolute, am prior to the root, the child and the beingness.

You eat different items of food to sustain yourself, which is your "childhood principle"—the beingness. When it disappears, you will be termed "dead." Actually what are you protecting from death? It is the basic "child-beingness"—the root. With the emergence of the child begins the first day of experiencing.

V: Is the state prior to beingness experienced consciously by Maharaj?

M: In that state "I" alone prevail without even the message "I am." There are no experiences at all. It is the non-experiential eternal state.

V: How will I know that you know it from your direct experience and not from a book?

M: I repeat, I alone do prevail in the state; hence, there is no otherness. For any experience, otherness is necessary.

---

1 By "them," the visitor is apparently referring to both the beingness and non-beingness states.

V: But that is true for everybody. Some know it; some do not.

M: Why should I bother about others? Who else is there? In that state of "Aloneness," "I" only exist.

V: How is that state to be cognized?

M: When the state of beingness is totally swallowed, whatever remains is that eternal "I."

V: Because that Absolute "I" state felt alone, it occurred to it "I am lonely, let me be many"—as referred to in the *Chandogya Upanishad*.

M: This can occur at the threshold of beingness. But since my ultimate state is beyond the grasp of the *Upanishads*, I reject them. The *Upanishads* are the storehouse of knowledge, which however has emanated from the state of ignorance. The raw material used for presenting the teachings is ignorance only.

All the three *gunas* are bound by and charged with emotions, but are not the truth. Because of the creation of this fraudulent world, out of "spit," people are veritably ashamed. Therefore, they do not like to expose the offender through which the "spit" was ejected. Considering this aspect, how can you have ego at all? From where have you emerged and where are you proceeding to?

V: From nowhere to nowhere.

M: When such profound discussions are going on, only the fortunate ones will be present. [*To the visitor who asked questions:*] Here your self-esteem is fully exposed. Do you like that?

V: I have nothing to hide. You told me to stand up and fight.

[*Maharaj recites a couplet from a folk song normally sung by dancing girls touring the countryside. The song, with deep meaning, was composed by a famous sage some centuries back:*]

Having had many a lover,
I made them dance and they pined for me.
But in my guru, I met a perfect match.
He made me dance to the tune he played.
Oh, my friends, listen:
Beware of a perfect guru.
Once you meet him, where would you be
With your ego-sense totally wiped out.

Kabir, the great poet-sage, says in a verse:
    I recited the sacred names, a million times;
    performed austerities and penances
    But I did not realize myself.
    When I met the perfect Master, Niranjan—the
                Unblemished
    Instantly I realized the Highest
    And abided in the state of Non-Attention—*alak*.[2]

January 16th 1980

---

2 The state before conception. For further elucidation of the state of *alak*, see Maharaj's discussion of the borderline between being and 'non-being' on pp. 4 and 67

6.

THE NECTAR OF THE LORD'S FEET

MAHARAJ: If one obtains and relishes the nectar of the Lord's feet,[1] the *charan-amrita*, the mind can be conquered. This means that the mind will no longer hold sway over us; its mastery imposed from childhood will no longer oppress us. This is called *manojaya*—victory over the mind. But this is made possible only with His Grace. Without Grace, we cannot relish the nectar.

However, only a true devotee, a *bhakta*, a god, can obtain the *charan-amrita*. But who and what is this devotee? It is nothing else but the consciousness, the sense of being, the knowledge that "we are," which has appeared unknowingly and spontaneously in us. The consciousness is the *charan-amrita*, the nectar of the Lord's feet.

The entire cosmos in its vibrant, stirring movement is represented by the consciousness, the feet of the Lord, and the whole universe is the body of the consciousness. But what is its relationship with all beings? It dwells in the core of all beings as the knowledge "I am," the love "to be," the *charan-amrita*.

---

1 In this talk, Maharaj does not go into the origin of this expression, but its meaning becomes clear from what Maharaj stated on another occasion: "Why are the feet of the guru honoured? Because they bring you to the Absolute."

One who drinks the nectar of the Lord's feet is a true devotee. He abides in the knowledge "I am." He is godly. Thus, when one sips continuously this nectar by witnessing the consciousness or the sense of being, one's mind, which assesses and differentiates persons observed as males and females, gradually removes itself from the focus of attention, leaving the consciousness in its innate glory.

But how can such a state be attained? Only if one totally accepts the knowledge "I am" as oneself with full conviction and faith and firmly believes in the dictum "I am that by which I know 'I am'." This knowledge "I am" is the *charan-amrita*. Why is it called *amrita*—the nectar? Because, it is said, by drinking nectar one becomes immortal. Thus, a true devotee, by abiding in the knowledge "I am" transcends the experience of death and attains immortality. But so long as the mind remains unconquered, the experience of death is inevitable.

Although my talks go on and on with many visitors, my standpoint remains unchanged. Why? Because my standpoint is stabilized at the *charan-amrita*. It stays put in the consciousness, the source of concepts and language. Out of it emanates the language from its subtlest formation to the grossest vocal expression, as *para, pashyanti, madhyama,* and *vaikhari.*

If you could just give up all other spiritual efforts and disciplines and absorb yourself in relishing the *charan-amrita,* by abidance in the consciousness, the mind will release you from its clutches. At present, you meekly accept whatever the mind dictates as your own. If the mind goes into silence, where and what are you?

Once you subside into the consciousness, the factual state of Reality shall be revealed to you with the knowledge that will emanate out of you intuitively, like spring water. This will enable you to discern not what is real and unreal, but most importantly, to realize what "I am."

What am I for myself alone? What is this life? Once these

questions are resolved intuitively and the Reality emerges, the mind cannot predominate any longer. However, functioning of the mind will go on, but the quality of its functioning will be totally different. One who has attained such a state remains unaffected by any happenings, since the blabberings of the mind can have no effect. And who could be that one? Surely not an individual who is trapped in the mind-shell. But that one is the knowledge "I am"—the consciousness.

It is said that we should break off the shackles that attach us to the body and the world. What does that mean? Whatever is seen and perceived is at the bodily or worldly level. An attachment is developed with objects perceived, and then we identify with a body as ourselves and claim the objects as our own. Attachment is the nature of the mind, and it obstinately persists in these attachments. But if you drink the *charanamrita* by stabilizing in the consciousness, everything will be resolved and you will be enlightened. You need not go to anybody to clear your doubts.

While doing my normal chores and singing *bhajans* in praise of God and so on, to you I appear to be deeply involved in these activities. But actually I remain apart from myself, bereft of the body and mind sense, and then witnessing of the activities happens to Me. I wonder if you have marked this! Many persons are related to me in some way or another. Although seemingly I hobnob with them, I am apart from them. For myself, I have fully realized what "I am," and right now it is absolutely clear to me what and how "I am." But what these persons think "they are," only they know. They presume to have acquired knowledge, to have reached a spiritual status higher than others...and so forth. This is bound to be, because they are still slaves to their mind. In my case, it cannot happen. I have totally imbibed the nectar of the Lord's feet—the consciousness.

At present, all communications and functionings happen through the medium of this nectar—the consciousness. And what is this medium? It is the knowledge "I am." It is repre-

sented by Lord Vishnu, the highest god who reclines blissfully on the coils of the serpent, *sheshashayi*, and hence is
known as *sheshashayi-Bhagavan*.

Well, it is nice to have such talks, but to imbibe and realize their essence is very difficult indeed. Why? Because you
firmly believe that you are the body and live accordingly,
while entertaining fond wishes that you will achieve something good in the world, and later still better. These expecta-
tions are primarily based on the misconceived notion that
you are the body. This wrong identification, however, dissolves in the nectar of the Lord's feet, when you totally subside in the consciousness and lose your individuality.

Dissolution of individuality is not possible without devotion to the Master—*guru-bhakti*—which in other words is
again the consciousness, the *guru-charan-amrita*. Abidance in
the consciousness removes all past and future problems, and
stabilizes one in the present—Here and Now.

Consciousness is the sense of knowingness "I am" without words, and it appeared unknowingly and unsolicited. It is
the manifest universal life force and, therefore, cannot be
individualistic. It extends inside and outside, like the brilliance of a diamond. You see a dream-world inside you and a
perceptible world outside you, provided the consciousness
prevails. From the body level, you may say inside and outside
the body, but from the standpoint of consciousness, where
and what is inside and outside? Only in the realm of knowingness "I am"—the consciousness—can a world be, and so
also an experience.

Hold on to this knowingness "I am," and the fount of
knowledge will well up within you, revealing the mystery of
the Universe; of your body and psyche; of the play of the five
elements, the three *gunas* and *prakriti-purush*; and of everything else. In the process of this revelation, your individualistic personality confined to the body shall expand into the
manifested universe, and it will be realized that you permeate
and embrace the entire cosmos as your "body" only. This is

known as the "Pure Superknowledge"—*shuddhavijnana*.

Nevertheless, even in the sublime *shuddhavijnana* state, the mind refuses to believe that it is a non-entity. But as one subsides in the consciousness, one develops a firm conviction that the knowledge "you are"—the sense of your being—is the very source of your world. This knowledge alone makes you feel "you are" and the world is. Actually, this manifest knowledge, having occupied and permeated the cosmos, dwells in you as the knowledge "you are." Hold on to this knowledge. Do not try to give it a name or a title.

Now coming to a very subtle situation, what is it in you that understands this knowledge "you are"—or from your standpoint "I am," without a name, title or word? Subside in that innermost centre and witness the knowledge "I am" and *just be*. This is the "bliss of being"—the *svarupananda*.

You derive pleasure and happiness through various external aids and processes. Some like to enjoy good food, some like to see a picture, some get absorbed in music...and so on. For all these enjoyments some outside factors are essential. But to abide in the "bliss of being" no external aids are required at all. To understand this, take the example of deep sleep. Once you are in deep sleep, no aids or treatments are called for and you enjoy a quiet happiness. Why? Because in that state identity with a body as male or female is totally forgotten.

Some visitors ask me, "Please show us a path that will lead to Reality." How can I? All paths lead to unreality. Paths are creations within the scope of knowledge. Therefore, paths and movements cannot transport you into Reality, because their function is to enmesh you within the dimension of knowledge, while the Reality prevails prior to it. To apprehend this, you must stay put at the source of your creation, at the beginning of the knowledge "I am." So long as you do not achieve this, you will be entangled in the chains forged by your mind and get enmeshed in those of others.

Therefore, I repeat, you stabilize at the source of your

being and then all the chains will snap asunder and you will be liberated. You will transcend time, with the result that you will be beyond the reach of its tentacles and you shall prevail in Eternity. And this sublime state can be attained only by drinking ceaselessly the nectar of the guru's sacred feet—the *guru-charan-amrita*. It is a state of ecstatic beatitude—the self subsiding blissfully in the Self. This ecstasy is beyond words; it is also awareness in total quietude.

The quintessence of the talk is clear. Your most important asset is the "knowledge" that "you are" prior to emanation of mind. Hold on to this "knowledge" and meditate. Nothing is superior to this, not even devotion to a guru—*guru-bhakti*—or devotion to God—*Ishwara-bhakti*.

January 25th 1980

7.

TO REALIZE THE ABSOLUTE, EVEN BEINGNESS HAS TO BE TRANSCENDED

MAHARAJ: Seen from the earth, the sun rises and sets. But from the standpoint of the sun, it shines continuously and has no knowledge of rising and setting. While the beingness and its manifestation, including the activities therein, are temporary and time-bound, that which is prior to beingness is eternal. You are a student of the *Bhagavad-gita*; whatever I say, does it agree with the Gita?

VISITOR: After listening to your talks I was able to understand clearly the fifteenth chapter of the Gita, where mention is made of *Purushottama*.

M: *Purushottama* is the Absolute, the Eternal. While the Absolute is without any external support, being totally self-supporting, it is itself the support for everything manifest.

V: Krishna has said: "Those alone who understand that I, the Absolute, am beyond the states of being and non-being realize my true nature, and all others are fools."

M: Those who are created out of stupid action are also stupid.

V: Whatever a *jnani* talks, is spiritual knowledge and even his behavior reveals knowledge.

M: Actually all our behavior is of the *sattva-guna* quality expressed out of the food essence, and it is neither yours nor mine. The *sattva-guna* has three states, viz. waking, deep sleep and beingness. When knowledge is correctly understood one is pure Brahman only, though having a body form.

It has no mind-modification.[1] This is what Krishna said.

The body is a product of the food essence. All plants, shrubs, trees, animals etc. are created out of seeds, and a seed (*bija*) means re-creating in the previous form. Also a seed is a product of the *sattva-guna*. Out of a seed sprouts the plant and later a big tree, but the source is the seed only.

Also out of the human seed, which is the product of the three *gunas* (*sattvas*, *rajas* and *tamas*) and the food essence, sprouts the body, beingness and manifestation. This can be realized by a human being only.

Having understood this, I have realized pure Brahman though having a body form. Rarely, anybody imbibes this wisdom. Many acquire so-called knowledge, but whatever is acquired is not true knowledge.

V: Is the beingness, or the knowledge "I am," then the ultimate, true knowledge?

---

1 Reduced to its simplest terms, one might say that the mind undisturbed by thoughts—in a state of total peace and purity—is the *sattva guna*. In this mode, the mind is not different from the Self. The mental modifications (*vrittis*) are the perturbations of mind that result from the interplay of *tamas* and *rajas*; these cause man to lose sight of the fact that he is the Self and need not make any effort to gain it. Ramana Maharshi said much the same thing when he stated: "The common man is aware of himself only when modifications arise in the intellect; these . . . are transient—they rise and set. When pure awareness is left over, it is itself the *chit* (Self) or the Supreme." (*Talks with Sri Ramana Maharshi*, 7th edition, 1984, page 587.)

M: This true knowledge, the knowledge "I am," is also rendered the status of "non-knowledge" in the final Absolute state. When one is established in his final free state, the knowledge "I am" becomes "non-knowledge."

When you see a flowering tree you look only at the foliage, but you do not think of its roots and the seed out of which it has sprouted. Unless you understand the seed also, there will be no total understanding.

At present you understand yourself as a body, but you do not include in the understanding the source and the seed out of which this body has manifested.

A pen-point moist with ink writes volume after volume. The pen-point is the source of all writings. Similarly, your beingness is the source and beginning of your entire world.

The written material is easily observed and read, but its source—the pen-point, which is almost dimensionless—is not easily perceived. So also is the seed-beingness, which is formless, most elusive.

You do not identify with your beingness, but you are quick to identify with your visible body form. You cling to the form as "I" instead of the beingness. However, for the sustenance of the beingness a body form is essential. Even if Lord Krishna were to decide to incarnate again, he would be able to do so only with the medium of seed-beingness, which however will be a product of a food-essence body.

Not only Krishna, but also Christ and Buddha manifest only through the food-essence beingness. But do you know the meaning of Buddha, the *bodhisattva*?

V: Buddha means the innate nature of all of us.

M: And when you were initiated, what was the form of initiation and what were you initiated into?

V: I was taken into the order of holy *sangh*, as a monk, who was working for total happiness ...

M: Do not tell me all this. *Diksha* (initiation) means "just be," alertly "Be what you are." What advice was given to you at the time of initiation?

V: To watch my body-mind.

M: From what standpoint, or identity, did you watch?

V: I did not watch my body from any standpoint. There was only watching.

M: When you do not know yourself, then who is watching? And how does it happen?

V: The object of my witnessing comes up in the observer. Through the object comprising thought-emotion and body, there is a sense of self. I could observe this sense of self. I have seen pretty clearly that there is nothing substantial within this mind-body process.

M: How were you asked to be alert at the time of initiations?

V: All the time.

M: But with what identity should you be alert?

V: They did not tell me about any identity. They told me to be just alert.

M: To whom did they tell? Should they not indicate what the witness should be like?

V: No.

M: This is a lower type of initiation. First recognize the indwelling principle, the knowledge "I am" or the "self-love," which is doing the witnessing. The witnessing just happens to it. When the pain is there, spontaneously I witness the pain that I am experiencing.

V: There seems to be a sense of separation between myself and the object of witnessing. So when I witness ...

M: But when do you witness?

V: When I witness the body-mind, I feel separation from body-mind.

M: To whom does the witnessing happen?

V: That I do not know.

M: Then what type of spirituality do you practice?

V: Though I wear a robe, I do not follow any particular avenue of spirituality or order. I just try to be aware of who I am.

M: For all beings it is the same experience. Early morning, immediately after waking, just the feeling "I am" is felt inside or the beingness happens, and thereafter further witnessing of all else happens. The first witnessing is that of "I am." This primary witnessing is the prerequisite for all further witnessing. But to whom is the witnessing occurring? One that ever is, even without waking, to that ever-present substratum the witnessing of the waking state happens. The mystery of world-experience is at this point. The esoteric knowledge of seed-beingness is also here. Now you have woken up, and witnessing of waking happens. The primary witnessing is of my own presence, my existence. This waking, or the sense of existence, is a temporary state, being one of the trio of the deep-sleep, waking and knowingness states which together constitute the beingness. This beingness is like that quality of the moist pen-point. The aggregate of these three is the subtle energy represented by the male and female principles, termed *purushaprakriti*. In this beingness, the *sattva-guna*, is the *visvasutra*, *brahma-sutra*, *atma-sutra*. In that beingness dwells the universal manifestation. This *sattva-guna* is the thread around which Brahman and the manifest universe are strung.

V: A question I want . . .

M: What questions could you possibly have on this subject?

The very focus of that wet pen-point has assumed the multifarious forms. That beingness is known as *sattva-shakti* and *prakriti-purushashakti*. The *sattva-guna* which gave rise to the beingness is the product of the essence of the parents who belong to the species of *vachaspati*. This very essence assumed form, and the universe is revealed in its inside and outside. Understand clearly the source. It is just like a tiny seed of a banyan tree growing into a magnificent tree and occupying a lot of space, but who is it that occupies the space? It is the power of that small seed. Similarly, understand this quintessential emission of the parents that leads to the touch of "I-am-ness," which manifests itself into a universe. Therefore go to that source and understand it fully. Just as the seed carries the latent form of the plant, so the seed of the parents carries the latent form of male or female in the image of the parents.

Father and mother are also the expression of the *sattva-guna*, the quintessential principle only. As a result of friction, emission has taken place. This emission having taken the photo of the parents grows into a child in the likeness of the parents. Before your birth, where was your beingness dwelling dormantly? Was it not in the quintessence of the parents? Is this not the eternal drama of reproduction of all species through the *sattva* principle and the energy denoted by *purushaprakriti*?

V: The touch of "I-am-ness" is itself nothing personal; it seems personal only when linked with body and mind.

M: This touch of "I-am-ness" is the manifest only and is not individualistic.

V: You talked about the "I-love" state. If I say I love somebody, it really means "I-am-ness" on this spot recognizes "I-am-ness" on that spot.

M: There is no otherness at all to make love to. Only the "love to be" has sprouted. To sustain the "love to be" state, you undergo a lot of difficulties and adversities. Just to keep that state pleased and satisfied, you involve yourself in so many activities.

V: The suffering is to direct attention to something other than the "I love" state, but if all this is meant to perpetuate "I-am-ness," then is this not a desire?

M: This is not desire, it is the very nature of "I-am-ness" to be. Beingness wants to be and perpetuate itself. This is its very nature; it is not the individual's nature.

V: Even when it is linked with body-mind?

M: A number of minds and bodies are formed out of that principle. It is the source of creation. Millions of species are created out of that basic principle. It is *moolamaya*, the seed-illusion.

V: Is "I am" creating you?

M: Out of my beingness are created the three worlds. In my dream-world millions of worms, human beings etc. are created. When and from where did that dream-world emerge? It emerged from the apparent waking in the dream state.

V: If I close my eyes, does it mean that you do not exist?

M: Who told you that your eyes are closed?

V: My "I-am-ness."

M: When you shut your eyes, was your consciousness also shut?

V: No.

M: As a result of the love union of embodied objects termed as parents, you are the reminder that you are the creation resulting from their blissful moment. The memory, "I am," reminds of the blissful moment. This form, the embodied person, is a reminder of the bliss. You have collected a lot of knowledge, and you think yourself fit to be a guru and then you will expound the knowledge—that is, the collected knowledge, and not the revealed knowledge of your own. The knowledge is not fully revealed to you, you have not realized yourself, and hence you will be pseudo-gurus. Your existence was in a dormant condition in your father and mother. Now you want to proceed somewhere from here. From where did you spring? Go to the source from which you emerged. Be there first. Somebody had the fun of bliss and I suffer and cry for a hundred years.

V: Is it correct to compare "I-am-ness" to a room with two doors? On one side you see the world, and out of the other you perceive *Parabrahman*.

M: There are no doors to *Parabrahman*, dear son. Look at the door from which you emerged. Before emerging out of that door, how and where were you? You can put questions relating to this subject.

V: There is love and suffering too, in this "I am."

M: The cause is happiness, and the result is "I-am-ness."
    The cause is bliss, but the outcome has to suffer from the beginning till the end.

V: In that passing moment is there awareness of love and suffering simultaneously?

M: Everything that prevails in the cosmos at the time of love is registered in the outcome; and, incidentally, the outcome takes the form, is a replica, of the parents. Your birth means a film of the universe at that time. It is not merely a birth, it is charged with universe inside and outside.

V: Once you are born, consciousness is continuous, but in my meditation it comes and goes.

M: Beingness is continuous and it knows itself only with the aid of a body form, while without it, it does not know itself (i.e., it is in the Absolute state). Who is the witness of the coming and going of the consciousness?

V: Just awareness.

M: What you say is correct in a way, but actually it is not so.
    It is like saying that I promise to give you ten thousand rupees, but...The awareness is the *Parabrahman* state, but it is only a word; you have to abide in that state. At present, "I am" is in the beingness state. But when I do not have the knowingness of the "I am" illusion, then the *Poornabrahman* or *Parabrahman* state prevails. In the absence of the touch of "I-am-ness," I am the total complete *Poornabrahman* state, the permanent state.
    The borderline of beingness and non-beingness is intellect-boggling, because the intellect subsides at that precise

location. This borderline is the *maha-yoga*.

In the phrase "you and I," once the conjunction "and" is removed, no duality exists—that is, there is no separateness of "you" and "I." Similarly, this beingness is like a conjunction: when it is removed, no duality remains.

You must be at that borderline, that *maha-yoga* state. You descend into the *godown*² of that state which has the title of "birth."

V: Where is the place of anger, fear and hate in that *godown*? In beingness, the birth principle, that touch of "I am"?

M: In the seed of those two forms (parents), there is potential for innumerable universes.

V: What you say very much agrees with the teachings of J. Krishnamurti.

M: The one who understands this speck of ignorance—that is beingness—can speak of anything he likes. In the space of that speck of beingness innumerable universes dwell. If you wish to understand this better, take the example of a dream-world. This dream-world is nothing but the apparent waking state in deep sleep, of very short duration—it is like touch and go. In the dream a lot of dream-universes are created.

January 28th 1980

---

2 Oriental warehouse.

8.

IN THE ABSENCE OF BODY IDENTITY, WHERE IS THE MIND?

MAHARAJ: There is no doer, there is no creator of this manifest world and universe. There is no enjoyer; all is happening spontaneously.

VISITOR: While doing *japa* (i.e., repetition of sacred words), should we bring the meaning of the words into the focus of attention?

M: You should not deliberately try to work out the meaning of the *japa*. Meaning will spread by itself in you, will charge you in due course according to your quality. Manifestation of the dynamic *shakti* or energy takes place through the person and varies with each individual. By all means perform your family activities, comply with worldly and social responsibilities with full zest and enthusiasm, but at least understand and know your own "self," what "you are." And gradually you will realize that as the knower you have no identity with respect to a place or form. All perceptible and tangible movements in the universe and world just happen, without any specific reason; that is, there is functioning, rotating, vibrating, humming, without a purpose. However, You prevail forever without identity of body form, name or any other illusory datum. And whatever the other principle is, defined by and identified with form, illusion, name and body, it creates, nourishes and sustains itself by itself. Later it has to disappear. Understanding all this action-play is knowledge. Lord Krishna only spoke about *Paramatman*—that is, the highest self—as himself. Others also expounded, but they were caught up in their own concepts. If I do any thinking at all, it relates to the manifestation and its natural play. I do not think of altering the course of manifestation. However, when you engage in thinking it will be at the personality or individual level, about your personal problems. There is nothing to be done, just find out how this touch of "I-am-ness" has come about in you.

V: When I talk, there is no feeling that I am talking.

M: Now you talk from whatever identity you have. What is the support of that identity?

V: The words just come out.

M: When you talk, do you depend on your own existence or someone else's?

V: On my own identity.

M: This beingness of the self is of a short duration; it is experienced for a short time only. But the one that experiences the beingness exists for ever. You must realize that the Experiencer, "You," is the ever-present, existing principle. From what identity are you going to talk?

V: Since I have absolutely no desire to talk, it does not come from the former.

M: I want a precise reply to my question. Why did you utter some irrelevant words? I again repeat my question, "Are you talking from the standpoint of the short-duration beingness, or the Eternal?"

V: There is no personal "I" that is talking.

M: Do not give me that! I accuse you that you alone are talking. Are you talking from the temporary position, or the permanent one?

V: Not from the temporary position.

M: You are not telling the truth.

V: It is my experience that no "I" is talking. When you say that "I," the person, is talking, it is not true.

M: You are silly to say this, as the true knowledge has not been revealed to you. Are you going to give me the information from the standpoint of the temporary phase or the other?
You do not seem to understand my question.

V: It shows clearly to me that what appears temporal is really temporal.

M: Then what type of information will you give someone about the state which is permanent?

V: I will insist that he should go and see a *sat-guru*.

M: Then where is the value or worth of the person who is guiding?

V: He will be a guide to some few people who will be visiting him.

M: I am going to send you out of here. I am not going to give you any knowledge. Should I teach you the ABC of all this? Read the book *I Am That* and ponder over it first. Every time a fellow comes here, am I to teach him from scratch? How was "I" prior to the appearance of beingness? How and why did the beingness appear? We must get the answers to those questions only.

V: I follow the approach shown by my guru. Whatever is acquired is unreal and time-bound.

M: This anybody can say. How did this body and beingness arise? I want to know that.

V: I have not decided what I should talk about. Whatever is imbibed by me will express itself.

M: Nobody can decide what he is going to talk about. Suppose you prepare yourself to talk a lot here, and cannot recollect it; then what? It is not as if whatever you decide is actually going to transpire every time. The sense that "you are" is a big thing. What is most significant is the fact that you remember your sense of being. Subsequently, all other things appear. Earlier this memory "I am" was not, and suddenly it appeared. Now I expound on the spiritual talk called *niroopona*. In Marathi the word *niroopona* is derived from the word *niroopa*, which means "message." Therefore, to deliver any spiritual talk that is *niroopona*, the primary message "I am" must first be present; then whatever ensues from this primary message will be the spiritual talk. The spiritual message which is delivered gives information about those who listen to the message. For delivering this message, the Absolute "I" assumes the beingness. Now take the case of a Government courier; he merely delivers a Government message, but, he is not the Government. He carries out his duty as a Government servant. But here the "I-am-ness" itself is the Gov-

ernment and the courier. Some prophets say they are mes-
sengers of God. But Krishna does not say that. He emphati-
cally declares "All this creation is out of Me, but I—the
Absolute—am apart from it. And whatever is created out of
me, blazes like the fireworks in a festival, and gets extinguished, but I—the Absolute—prevail for ever." There are different methods of expounding spirituality. I do not learn by
rote the spiritual pronouncements of others. The main point
to be understood is this. How and why did this sense of my
being appear, with the title of birth; and how was I, prior to
the sense of being? Only a very rare one understands this.

There have been many incarnations. But only Bhagavan
Krishna said, "I am the creator of all the *avatars* and I am
also their knower."

Both Shankaracharya and Ramana Maharshi have
explained this aspect of spirituality, with clarity. How am I
the eternal "I"? And how am "I," the one qualified by the
sense of beingness and time? This is to be understood. That
is all.

But the great *moolamaya* deludes you by influencing you
to believe that you have taken millions of births. But you, the
ignorant one, never ponder on this in a correct manner. Prior
to your birth, you had no knowledge that "you were" and that
you experienced millions of such births. Can such a story be
believed at all? You believe that you are born, and that you
have rebirths, don't you? What are you and how are you?
Unless attention is paid to this, and it is understood fully,
you will not be released from the domination of such concepts. They are also conveyed by the four Vedas, which have
made many persons dance to their tune. When I concentrated my attention on the point of waking, the Vedas folded
their palms in total surrender and went into silence.

To understand the process, consider first the *prakriti* and
purusha, the two eternal principles. As a result of their interaction, the five great elements and the three *gunas* have
emerged. Space, air, fire, water, together with *sattva*, *rajas*

and *tamas*, formed the earth, making it ready for further development. On the earth grew vegetation, and when the juice of the vegetation took body form, the dormant principle of beingness also appeared in it. The five elements have no inkling of their sense of being. The beingness is manifested in body form during the five-elemental process. From then on, rules, regulations, rituals etc. were formulated. Now that eternal principle, which did not know its existence, is manifest through millions of forms.

Before the birth, neither that principle nor the parents knew each other. The principle was planted in fluid form in the womb of the mother. In the course of nine months it developed into the form of an infant, who is the very seed of all future experiences. This seed-beingness is the pure *sattva*, and the quintessence of the food body, and it is wholly ignorance only. The seed of future experiences determines *prarabdha*, which is whatever that future child will have to suffer and experience. The unfortunate child, who was not in his "knowingness" before birth, is now presented with a whole gamut of sufferings at birth. At the moment of a child's conception, the exact photo of the total situation in the cosmos, including the material out of which he was created (parents), position of planets, stars in the firmament etc. was imprinted on him. What is that principle which takes the photograph? That supreme principle is known by titles such as *brahma-sutra*, *moolamaya*, *maha-tattva*, *hiranyagarbha*, *atma-prem* etc. It is called *maha-tattva*[1] because it has supreme significance in the world. This *maha-tattva* is further known by godly names such as Christ, Krishna, Shiva, and Vishnu. It is also called *parabdhi*—that is, the ocean of life seething with millions of forms. Lord Krishna says that through this *yogamaya*, the Supreme Principle, I execute all the universal functions in the world, while, I, as Absolute, remain aloof.

The entire manifest universe is linked and charged with

---

1 Literally: 'Great Truth.'

this energy through *yogamaya*, the *yogashakti*. This beingness was not fully manifest in the womb. Therefore you remember that your "I-am-ness," your destiny, has appeared spontaneously and unsolicitedly. This beingness, which is manifest, how long is it going to last? It has brought with it its own expiration date; hence, it is time-bound. In the womb, the beingness does not know itself.

A *jnani* is called thusly because he understands the roots of beingness, and that it is pure ignorance only. He does not involve himself in the play of this beingness, and hence transcends it. He observes the sprouting, nourishing and disappearance of this principle, and knows he is not that principle. He is the witness and knower of that beingness, the *prarabdha*.

That beingness, which was in the nascent stage in the womb, felt its beingness a little after coming into the world and accepted the identity of its body as itself. Through nourishment, this form began to develop into the image of the parents whose photo was imprinted upon it at the time of conception. This little container of food essence is being sucked by that beingness, "I am," day and night. The principle that sucks that container is not the body, it is apart from the body. This beingness principle dwells in that food body itself. Just as the child sucks on the mother's breast, the beingness consumes the body.

You want self-knowledge, don't you? It is by no means child's play. If you want to be a *jnani*, you must understand what you are; that is, what this "I-am-ness" is and how it did appear. What was your true state prior to "I-am-ness"? Only Lord Krishna has expounded this clearly. He says, since "I-am-ness" appears and disappears, I, the Absolute, cannot be that. I forever prevail.

My *sat-guru* told me: "In spite of your worldly activities, you are unborn, you are apart from all." So any person can become a *jnani* provided he clearly understands the following: Beingness appears as a result of the food-essence body, functions by itself, and disappears when the quality of food body fails to sustain it. In the process of this understanding, he realizes that he is not the beingness, and so abides in the *jnani* state.

There have been so many incarnations who claimed the highest spiritual status, but they got stuck in concepts gathered from outside themselves—either by listening, or by reading books. To conduct any worldly or spiritual activities, words are necessary. Since a *jnani* transcends concepts, he is word-free. In the quietude of the *jnani*, the words went into silence, because the Vedas, while saying "I am not this, I am not that,"[2] exhausted totally all their words and became "Vedanta"—that is, the end of Vedas, end of words.

I have told you enough about the *prarabdha* and its experiences, and how and why they were created. Now in this whole play, where are you? What is your location? What is your identity that you would like to preserve? What identity of yours right from childhood until now has remained faithful to you? Once, you had the identity of a child, followed by that of youth, then of middle age, finally that of an old man. Amongst all these, which is your one true identity? As a matter of fact, there is no evidence at all that you were born.

V: I do not think of any identity as such. In all my experience, at times I feel the sense of "I" much less. It is just attention and object of attention. But when the attention is on "I am," then "I am" becomes less.

M: When you put your attention on "I am," do you feel any physical sensation?

V: When my attention is not on "I am," it is gone. But when my attention is very strong, objects are perceived.

M: But is your attention stable, permanently?

---

2 Referring to the famous expression *neti-neti*; total negation in order to arrive at what one *is*.

V: Yes.

M: If so, describe that. And do you have this experience?

V: Yes.

M: Then, why did you come here?

V: The experience is not continuous.

M: If it is firmly stabilized, then it must be continuous and forever.

V: It is stable for a moment.

M: Who witnesses the two states of pure and impure attention?

V: Maybe the knower, the attention. Perhaps someone remarks on attention, but I do not speak.

M: Who is paying attention to all this, you or somebody else?

V: The truth knows.

M: You study it properly. Do meditation as often as possible. Go into *samadhi* for hours at a time.

V: My mind is still, but it is attentive. I look at this "I am."

M: You have come up to the stage of knowingness, but you still have to reach your destination. This is possible only when attention merges into attention. If it had expended itself, you would not have come here.

V: Oh, I see I should have chewed up my attention.

M: Yes. Currently, you are stagnating at the stage of attention. It should be fully consumed. You are now talking from that stage of knowledge, "I am," which is time-bound and temporary.

SECOND VISITOR: Objectless attention, could it be that?

M: Can that attention be, without any object? If attention is there, the object is also there.

V: When attention and its object fade out, then can one attain *samadhi*?

M: Who is the knower of it?

V: You are laying a bait for me?

M: Talk for yourself.

SECOND VISITOR: My mind is very still, and it is not moving towards any object; it seems to be a stillness of mind, a quietude. This is the result of my experiences here.

M: What did he say?

V: When something comes to feel that attention, my stillness is broken and the sense of "I am" comes into being. At that moment, my mind looks out towards the object, so that the object and the sense "I am" arise at the same time.

M: You appear to be talking from the body-mind state. I am talking from the no-mind state. The mind persists so long as the body-identity is there. When this is gone, where is the mind? The waking state, deep sleep and beingness are titled by the term "birth," and it is a temporary phase.

V: But don't I have to investigate the body-mind from that state in order to know it?

M: Am I a kindergarten teacher, that I should start from A, B, C—that is, the body-mind state? My talk begins from *prarabdha* and the root of beingness. I don't deal with body-mind.

January 31st 1980

9.

THROUGH THE TOUCH OF BEINGNESS, THE ENTIRE COSMOS ARISES

MAHARAJ: Whatever is seen and felt in totality, space-like, is universal manifestation—the Brahman. But "forms" emanated, and these are felt as separate and isolated from each other.

For a *jnani* everything is the Brahman—its expression only. Each living being has the sense of presence. This sense identifies itself with the body form and thus functions in the world. The sense of presence of being has tremendous potential, particularly in the human body, because the body senses in this species are developed to the highest degree.

This sense of being, which is the consciousness, has the capacity to realize its true nature and abide in the Ishwara state—that is, the godly state. The ancient scriptures, the four Vedas, have affirmed the sense of being as the pure Brahman only, which is also vouched for by the sages and saints.

The spray of the ocean contains innumerable droplets. But they are the ocean only when not separated from the ocean. On separation they are individual drops. Nevertheless, the salty taste of the water, whether of the ocean or of its droplets, is the same. Just as the salty taste is present in the entire ocean, the beingness or the sense of "I am" in the human form has the inherent capacity to be all-pervading. But having conditioned—and thereby limited—itself to the body form, it is interested only in protecting and preserving the body.

As a result of the arising of body forms, the manifest consciousness apparently was fragmented. But this fragmentation should be viewed only with respect to the body forms because in actuality the consciousness prevails, both within and without the bodies.

The mind is the outflow of the five vital energies[1] in the body, known as the *pancha-pranas*. It glorifies in, and gloats over, the impressions—the *samskaras*—which are received from the outside through the body senses. But the mind can purify itself in the association of sages and saints, who for this purpose commend the practice of chanting the sacred names of God, doing penance etc.

As a matter of natural phenomenon, the pure dynamic Brahman unknowingly wears various bodies, like garments, and then functions through them. This results in perception of the world taking place through the senses of the bodies. But into the bargain the indwelling principle—that is, the sense of "I-am-ness"—embraces the body as itself and acts in response to the dictates and demands of the body. But in spite of all these distortions and modifications, the sense of "I-am-ness" remains unchanged in its inherent nature. The very moment that this pure dynamic Brahman, which is the motive force behind the body's functioning, discontinues its impetus, the body goes into disorder, commonly termed as "death."

Thus, the consciousness does not go anywhere; merely its functioning through the "dead" body is extinguished then and there, and the pure dynamic Brahman remains unaffected.

---

1 In Hindu philosophy, the *prana* (Sanskrit for "breath"), the primal energy or vital breath, divides itself fivefold. "As a king employs officials to rule over different portions of his kingdom, so *prana* associates with himself four other *pranas*, each a portion of himself and each assigned a separate function." (*Prasna Upanishad*) The other four pranas are: *apana, samana, vyana,* and *udana*. The *pranas* are the essential enery component in such physiological functions as breathing, digestion and assimilation of food, excretion, and procreation.

As long as the sense of being or the consciousness dwelling in the body does not realize its true nature, it is bound to identify with the body and all its actions by claiming doership. But as a result of this claim, it is subjected to intense suffering when the body goes into disintegration and approaches death.

In a healthy body, movement of the vital breath is clearly felt. But when death occurs, the vital breath quits the body and movement stops instantly. However, in the case of the Brahman, there is no question of movement at all and it continues to be omnipresent. The point to be clearly understood is that when a body dies, this basic principle—the pure Brahman—does not leave and proceed anywhere, as an individual entity, simply because it ever pervades everything and everywhere. But, at the moment of "death" of the body, its expression through that body subsides then and there only.

When a musical instrument is played, the sound emanating from it fills the space around. But the moment the instrument stops playing, the sound does not travel anywhere; it diminishes and comes to an end.

At present, this body form is the product of the five elements. These elements are created out of the *atman*. But how does one recognize this *atman*? It is by understanding the knowledge "I am"—the *atma-jnana*. Just as space is all-pervading, so the knowledge "I am" is all-pervading, limitless and infinite. How strange, such a supreme principle is treated as though it is a body! All the sufferings are due to this mistaken identity. If you give the highest honor due to it, you will not undergo either suffering or death.

Birth and death are hearsays. A birth indicates the birth of a body; the latter is made up of food juices. There is no question of the *atman* needing to enter the body since it is already everywhere, like the sky. If a body is healthy, its functioning will start naturally because of the prevalence of the *atman*-principle. This principle is immortal and indestructible. If you want to get a taste of it, understand clearly that it is nothing other than the knowledge "you are," the touch of "I-am-ness." Do not forget this basic principle.

This great principle—the *atman*—remains unaffected by whatever actions you do from your body-identity. Nevertheless, the touch of "I-am-ness" appears only when a food-body is available. When you state "I am very strong and healthy," it means that plenty of wholesome food has been consumed and digested by you to make your body strong. But the body is not your sense of being. Even though it is strong, it has to be replenished daily with food and water. The vital breath, without lips and tongue, chews and sucks food essences from the body, while the mind sings in praise of the impressions collected externally through the body senses. And you in turn feel as if you are doing all these activities and claim them as "yours."

Let us call the sense of being the *guna*—that is, the quality or *jnana*—which means the knowledge "I am." This *guna* or *jnana* exists always latently in a food particle. So whenever a food-form is available, this latent quality manifests itself—with movement and pulsation initially, and as mind later.

The supreme all-pervading principle whose expression through a body is called *guna* is named as *sagunabrahman* in the Vedas. The name has several meanings like "love to be," sense of "I-am-ness," beingness etc. This state has no form or shape, as even the mind has no shape. Only a food-body has form.

This very principle expresses itself as worms and germs out of a decomposed human body. Whenever surplus food is thrown out and allowed to decompose, you will find live forms crawling in and out of it. The life-giving, dynamic *sagunabrahman* gives animation to food-forms, whenever conditions are conducive; but its expression varies according to the forms. Thus, we recognize these as worms, insects, birds, animals and so on, by their very shapes.

The very *sagunabrahman*, when manifested through a human body, has the potential to lead a seeker to the Highest, provided it is understood and realized correctly. And the *sagunabrahman* is nothing else but your sense of being and dwells in every human body. By abidance in this state, birth and death will be transcended. For this purpose you do not have to practice any rituals or spiritual disciplines. Only be prior to mind, just *be*.

Many persons are busy in the name of spirituality, in doing penances, chanting sacred names, making pilgrimages and pursuing other disciplines for their salvation. Let them do whatever they want. Probably they are required to cleanse away the sins of their past births according to their *prarabdha*.

If you happen to come across a sage who has realized his true nature, you will not be required to do anything in the way of spiritual disciplines. This is because through his teachings, he will reveal your true nature, as by placing a mirror before you.

Many so-called sages move from place to place propagating their spiritual knowledge. But why should I roam about and where? In my true state I am everywhere. This will be realized by you also when you abide in the knowledge "I am."

You go to your uncle or cousin because you are related to them through your body. But if you are everywhere, why should you go about? If you imbibe fully whatever I have expounded, no more spiritual disciplines will be required of you.

With this understanding you will observe and conclude that whatever spiritual and worldly activities are happening through you, they are merely entertainments for passing time, and that they are the functioning of the manifest dynamic principle only—the *maya*.

To abide in the knowledge "I am" is one's true religion—the *svadharma*. But instead of following it, you opted to be irreligious by submitting to the dictates of your concepts, which led you to believe that you are a body. This misconception ensured only the fear of death.

If food is not supplied to your body, it will grow weaker and weaker and one day your vital breath will leave the body. People will pronounce you dead, but you will not have the information. It may be that you are sinful, but this is only in respect of your identity as a body; so also your death refers to the body identity.

Please apprehend this clearly that You—the Absolute— bereft of any body identity, are complete, perfect and the Unborn. But you are accused of millions of births in past lives. In this connection, could you tell me at least one of your past births, if you remember? Do not go by what others say, but speak honestly of your own, direct experience only. As a matter of fact, you never had any birth. Various forms are appearing and disappearing as a result of the five-elemental play. In this play where are you and what are you? And where is the question of your coming and going? What are these religions and cults? Are they not merely the propagation of the fond ideas of sages and prophets to whom certain spiritual concepts occurred? And this could happen because the sages and prophets recognized the sense of being initially. Then they meditated and abided in it and finally transcended it, resulting in their ultimate realization. Thereafter, whatever knowledge sprouted out of them spontaneously became the religions and cults of their followers, because of their deep emotional involvement.

The most important fact to be understood is only this. If the touch of beingness is, then everything is. If the beingness is not, the world is not, the cosmos is not and nothing is there.

Have you any questions now?

VISITOR: You talked about the beingness sustained by the food-body, and about the dynamic manifest consciousness. Are they the same?

M: Both mean the same. There is no form or shape for this principle, just as the vital breath has no form, which is, however, dynamic and pulsating. The vital breath alone gives animation to the body and it will operate so long as the body is healthy.

Whatever is seen and perceived is continuously in a state of creation and destruction, but You in your true nature are unborn and indestructible. Unless you realize your true nature, there will be no peace for you.

No matter how much you strive to acquire any worldly gains, they are bound to go; so also your concepts and various identities. Even if you follow any religion in the hope of obtaining something permanent from the outside, you will be sorely disappointed. The main purpose of true spirituality is to liberate oneself completely from one's concepts and conditionings.

By following any religion, cult or creed, one becomes inevitably conditioned, because one is obliged to conform and accept its disciplines, both physical and mental. One may get a little peace for some time, but such a peace will not last long. In your true nature, you are the knower of concepts and therefore prior to them.

V: A dead body is lying on the ground. And since the manifest Brahman is everywhere, it could not have left the body. Then what is that principle that left the body to make it dead?

M: Let us regard the Brahman as space for the purpose of this discussion. Can the space be confined within the body? Next tell me, where did the death (of that body) begin in the all-pervading space? Is that possible?

What sort of a question did you ask? You'd better reframe your question to make it sensible.

V: In the living body there should be something other than space!

M: Other than space?

V: Space is there.

M: In the space, a lump of food was there and out of this food a body was formed. The manifest Brahman, which we have called space, expresses itself through the healthy food-body. You are inclined to call it *atman*. But the *atman* is not created like a body; it is the unborn principle, the Brahman.

V: Oh, that means *atman* is never created!

M: Certainly, *atman* has no birth. It is through the all-pervading Brahman that the body, together with the vital breath, functions. And then you interpret the process as the birth of *atman*.

All this expounding is only for those who have a genuine urge to understand spirituality. For others who are anxious to better their worldly lives, worshipping of various gods is recommended.

When a healthy body and vital breath (*prana*) function together, the sense of beingness expresses itself by putting into operation the limbs and senses of the body. This expression is an advertisement, which declares the eternal existence of the ultimate principle—the Absolute—the *Parabrahman*. When the body dies, the sense of beingness disappears and so there is no advertisement of the Absolute through the dead body; nevertheless, the Absolute continues to prevail as ever.

V: That is what I wanted to know.

M: A seeker was advised by a guru with the words "Look back." And the simple-minded seeker looked behind, taking the command literally, so the guru told him again, "Understand the meaning underlying the words. Understand your state prior to the present one. Go to the source. Look back. Recede."

You accept a concept and stop at it. Thus, your spiritual progress stagnates at the conceptual level.

You indicated your identity at various stages of your life by such concepts as "a child," "a boy," "a youth," "a middle-aged man" etc. But which conceptual identity of yours remained faithful to you? All the identities, in the course of time, proved illusory. Even the very principle behind the identities, that is the sense of your beingness, will prove illusory. Since it has appeared, it has to disappear; therefore, it is temporary and time-bound. But the knower of the beingness is the eternal Absolute.

Whatever experience you undergo is imperfect. Nevertheless, you will continue some spiritual practice, because the mind will not allow you to be quiet.

For the purpose of acquiring knowledge and to know the Brahman, you meditate on something. But what is your identity as a meditator? You are neither the meditation nor the object of meditation. Whatever it may be, You, which is apart from meditation and its object, are the Perfect, the Totality, the Eternal-Absolute.

February 2nd 1980

10.

WHEREVER IS FOOD,
THEREIN DWELLS THAT

ISITOR: To me the consciousness appears and disappears.

MAHARAJ: You are telling a lie. How can you know that the consciousness is not? Only in sleep, the consciousness is not. From the moment of waking to the moment of sleeping, the consciousness is there. Whenever you observe an object, the mind has to be there to interpret it. With consciousness the mind is there to perceive.

V: Whenever an object is seen, witnessing happens. I do not know what I should call this witnessing.

M: Without mind, there cannot be any witnessing. It can happen only when the objects of mind exist, which is predicated upon the presence of the consciousness. Primarily witnessing happens to the consciousness, in the realm of the mind. All the activities occur to the mind and intellect, and witnessing of that happens to the Self.

If the consciousness holds on to the body as its identity, then true knowledge will never dawn on you. The Self is given the guise of the body—hence the trouble.

V: There are many gurus and many paths. How do we select a right guru and a correct path?

M: Many visitors come here. And many of them are mainly interested in subjects connected with body and mind, but I am not interested in these topics. Rarely someone wants knowledge of the Self. My present subject matter is: Whatever is gone, does not vanish and die, but disperses and manifests into multiplicity. While the consciousness leaves the body, it remains ample, widespread and manifest.

In the manifest world, *avatars* and social workers have for thousands of years been trying to bring about a change. But in spite of their collective efforts, there has been no improvement at all. Human beings all have the same type of mind and intellect in which they are embroiled and caught up. But no improvement is possible in that state. I always go by the basic principle in the background. Unknowingly, everything is happening against that background, from that principle. A person is normally engaged in activities that may be considered good or bad, but are actually just mental occupation.

Everybody is trying to protect and preserve the time factor—that is, the consciousness. So long as time is there, consciousness is there; and time is there so long as the body is present.

When the life span is over, time has gone. When time has gone, consciousness is gone. As long as the beingness is there, activities proceed. Once you realize that you are not the body, then there is no more attraction for the manifestation.

When a firm conviction is established that one is not the body, one's behavior has become just like that of the five elements, claiming no credit as things are merely happening by themselves. Such a one can have no needs and demands.

Many people clothed in spiritual attitudes are not inclined to give up their bodily identity. In the name of spirituality, they go on pursuing creeds, faiths and disciplines. But they do not relinquish their cherished identity, nor do they proceed inwards towards their Self. All the diverse guises that are adopted are the characteristics of the mind—its various inclinations, latencies—and not those of the Self. Many people change creeds as some change wives when dictated by their mind.

When a butcher attains the realized state, he continues his vocation of slaughtering animals, because he knows that it is only the function of the body but that he is not the body and mind. He does not even need a God nor the knowledge of the Brahman.

Once you realize that you are not the body and the mind, you have no needs and demands; then you are one with the manifest consciousness. In due course you are not even the consciousness, when you dwell in the Highest, thus ultimately also transcending the consciousness. Manifest consciousness is the Brahman.

Once stabilized in the Brahman, there is no longer any use for knowledge of the Brahman—that is, knowledge of the Self. What can be the use of Brahman to the Brahman? Therefore, I, the Brahman, do nothing and need nothing, at this stage of *videhisthiti*, the body-free state. There is no high nor low; no real nor unreal; no inside nor outside and no dimension of any kind in that state.

In the name of spirituality, people adopt as their religion certain creeds and concepts and develop pride. Later, they give up all that and accept another creed, and so on. Finally, they will never know when their bodies "kick-off."

At present, you put your faith in the body. Once you give up that faith, you are the Brahman—the manifest principle. Bhagavan Krishna said, "Remember me, I am always there." What is that state of Krishna? He is beyond the body-mind state; that means, he is the consciousness. Further, Krishna as the Absolute is the witness of consciousness also; so whenever anybody thinks of him, it is of eternity only. In thinking thusly, a devotee himself dwells in eternity. Therefore Krishna says, "Remember me, memorize me." Do not use your identity with the body, but by all means use the body.

Although "I-am-ness" dwells in the body, it rejects the body as "I am not it." I, in the Krishna state, do not belong to the Hindu, Christian, or Muslim faith. Why? Because I am not the body and therefore I prevail in a Hindu, Christian, Muslim—in everyone and everything. Bring me a Muslim or a Christian without a body. Can you bring anyone like that? All religions and creeds are at the body-mind level. Is there any indwelling principle, such as Hindu, Christian, or Muslim, in the food we cultivate and consume? Thus, food does not provide any religious nourishment to indicate the religion of the person. A child of a Muslim food-body is considered a Muslim conventionally. This applies similarly to a child of a Hindu. Because the parents call themselves Hindu or Muslim, they impose their particular religion on their offspring. Could there be any religion, creed or faith in the food—a product of the five elements?

From the same eating place, people of different faiths consume a common food. But the moment the food is consumed by their body, it is given the religious status of that food-body. How strange!

In food, innately and dormantly, the sense of "I-am-ness" is already present. Once the food is consumed and assimilated in the body, the "I-am-ness" manifests itself.

With the appearance of a body, the necessity to assign a name is felt. We impose a name to identify that body, and then the very name is taken as the person. With the body, a form appears and with the form, a name to identify it. But how strange, the name is considered as the very person!

The world is full of children. Actually, they are products of food, and children yet to be born are already extant in the food essence though in a dormant state. When the food essence takes a form, it manifests a body, and the body provides sustenance to the indwelling "I am" principle. Just as milk is sucked by a child from a feeding bottle, so the food essence is consumed by the "I-am-ness" from the body. It is eaten and digested by the "I-am-ness" the whole day. With this understanding we should realize that we are not the body. This is liberation, and realization.

All of you are quiet now. Why? Because you are being cleared of your present identity, of your conviction that you are a body and mind. Therefore, you are unable to ask any questions.

To me, witnessing of the body-mind and beingness just happens. Now suppose some pain is felt due to some cause. Who understands it? It is the consciousness, which is sustained by the food-essence body. By "consciousness" I mean the universal consciousness only. But the witness of the consciousness is the highest principle—the Absolute.

The fragrance or sweetness of the food-essence body is the knowledge "I am." It has no name and form. It is the "I love" state, the "I"-taste. But from your body-mind state you will go to pilgrimages and various gurus. So long as the consciousness is there, that humming goes on, and who does the humming? The principle which is humming, and saying "I am, I am" is itself your guru.

If you imbibe what I say and understand this guru, the consciousness, and dwell there, you will be self-realized. Then no more rituals, disciplines and spirituality are necessary. Is it clear now to you what is termed "guru"? It is the sense of "I-am-ness."

In the devotional approach, worship is prescribed. In the ritual, *prasada* is prepared first, which is a food offering to the deity being worshipped. Before invoking the deity by ringing a bell, the *prasada* must be kept ready because God is sustained on food and the God is no one else but the consciousness, which depends on food.

Once a disciple, who had learned the art of bringing back to life the dead, saw a bone lying on his path while going through a forest. He felt like testing his skill on the bone, which happened to be that of a lion. So he began chanting mantras and performing the appropriate rituals. But he forgot to provide any offering. The bone materialized into a lion, who appeared quite hungry. So the animal looked all around for food and not finding any in its vicinity, roared ferociously and pounced upon the very disciple and gobbled him up.

Whenever food of the right quality and in the proper form is available and when the vital breath functions in it, the "I-am-ness" principle manifests itself through it. This "I-am-ness" is the Bhagavan—the godly principle.

During my wanderings, after meeting my guru, I once visited a holy place known as Pandharpur. This place is famous for the temple of God, Vithoba. I used to carry a staff, and to cover myself I only had a piece of loin cloth. On this occasion I stumbled upon a cremation ground. I was not interested in visiting temples, but I liked to see the temple architecture rather than the idols inside. Within the confines of that cremation ground, a skinny man was sitting in a corner. Out of curiosity, I approached him and queried, "Oh sir, why do you sit in this godforsaken place?" He replied, "Why do I sit here? I really do not know."

"Don't you visit the temple of Lord Vithoba?" I asked him further.

"No, why should I?" was his short reply.

"But, how do you manage for food?" I asked.

"Well, that is no problem. I eat the balls of food kept as offering for the dead bodies. And I use the cloth in which the bodies are wrapped to cover myself." He said this while I stood quite astonished at his naive replies, and continued:

"Why should I go anywhere for my needs? Wherever is food, therein dwells That."

These words carried a profound meaning, and I felt that he was spiritually quite an advanced soul.

Why should we go anywhere? Wherever there is food-form together with the vital breath, therein dwells the "Godly Principle." Therefore, I do not go anywhere. This Godly Principle is also called Bhagavan, the consciousness, the "I-am-ness" etc. and is praised by many names and titles.

After self-realization, any behavior or actions expressed through the body of a sage are spontaneous and totally unconditioned. They cannot be bound to any disciplines. A realized sage may be discovered in an unkempt person reclining in the ashes of a cremation ground, or on the cushioned bed in a palace as a king. He may be a butcher by vocation or a successful businessman. Nevertheless, a realized one, having transcended the realm of beingness, ever abides in the Eternal Absolute.

February 4th 1980

11.

EVEN THE HIGHEST IS USELESS TO THE HIGHEST

VISITOR: It seems to me that whenever a form is infused with life, consciousness is produced, which appears by reflection of awareness in matter. Should it not be the other way around?

MAHARAJ: Whatever you say is all right from the body-mind state. When the sense of being is cleansed from its body-mind state, then it is universal. This is the source for the creation of the five elements, three *gunas*, followed by the vegetable and animal kingdoms.

V: There is *prana*, the vital force in plants. Is there also consciousness in plants?

M: All that is seen and perceived in space is the creation of consciousness and is infused with it. The entire created world of form will finally merge into space. From the bodily standpoint, all forms appear as separate entities. But at the consciousness level, they are the consciousness-manifest and not separate.

As you make spiritual progress, you will realize that the source of the universe is your consciousness only. At present, you are in the grip of the discursive intellect, because of your identity with a body; therefore you are unable to understand. Whatever knowledge you now collect is from this identity, but that is not true knowledge. But when you have the knowledge about "what you are," you will understand that the very world and universe are contained in the speck of your consciousness only. At this stage you would have transcended your body-mind sense. But today, whatever knowledge you acquire is through your firm belief that you are the body-mind.

When you see the "inner" world as something external, you term it a "dream." But what is it that is perceived inside? It is contained in the sense that "you are," in your consciousness. Exactly the same process takes place in the waking state also.

Your consciousness, the sense of presence, is the very shell in which the waking world or the dream-world proliferates.

This is the actual state of affairs. But you accept all that you see with your body sense; and whatever you perceive is through the inadequate yardstick of your limited intellect. Whatever is visible or perceptible is an outcome of space only. When all that disappears, again space prevails. When your world concretizes out of space and in space, you term all that with various names and titles for your convenience, to carry out your day-to-day activities. In reality, no such names and titles exist. None of such creations has any authoritative, valid form or individuality of its own.

To realize this you must accomplish *jnana-yoga*, which means: the self subsiding in the Self. Again, *jnana-yoga* means to inquire how this "I-am-ness" and the world came about. To realize that "I-am-ness" and the world are one is *jnana-yoga*. Here, the knowledge "I am" should subside in itself.

But all you really want is to keep your body-mind sense intact; that just will not do. Thus, to realize that "I-am-ness" means the manifest world and the universe is the very fulfillment of *jnana-yoga*.

When the sense of being appears, it has no body sense. Out of that sense of being, the whole cosmos is created. In that creation you also have a form, but you accept body as your identity and move about and function in the world. The principle that motivates and enlivens the body is the sense of beingness only, but it is not the body. All this play in the cosmos and the world functions in the consciousness, and finally the play will merge into consciousness. Ponder over this without identifying with the body, and you, the consciousness, will know that accepting the form as identity is *maya*, illusion. Thus, the consciousness is the very seed-principle of the entire cosmos. It comprises the dynamic life force, *guna*, which is the quality of beingness, and *prana* or vital breath. Consciousness gives the knowledge that "you are." When the consciousness first appears it is free from identification of any kind with "this" or "that." Even though being the dynamic manifest universal principle, due to its identification with the body it suffers pain and pleasure. The consciousness knows itself through itself. Only a rare one realizes that the entire cosmos manifestation springs out of one's seed-consciousness. From *atma-yoga*, only *vis-vayoga*—that is, one's unity with the cosmos—is realized when one unites with oneself. The self abiding in the Self is the *jnana-yoga* which is a nameless and formless state, but later whatever manifests itself assumes a name and form. By merely acquiring knowledge one cannot claim to be a *jnani*. The *jnana-yogi* is not required to know anything as he is knowledge itself. *Jnana-yoga* is the highest state in spirituality. In this state there is no individuality, as this is the all-pervading state. Rarely will someone put a question from this standpoint and rarer still will there be someone who will answer these questions. The sense of individuality and needs are felt prior to *jnana-yoga*. But after the accomplishment of *jnana-yoga*, one is beyond needs and individual personality. *Kundalini-yoga* experts revel in the visions and powers obtained through yoga but will not expound the source of *kundalini* energy.

V: I quite agree that we shall reach the highest level. But you have said that from the highest suddenly springs "I-am-ness." Thus we are at the root of a total mystery.

M: What is the source prompting you to speak of levels and to think of reaching the highest level?

Level is only a concept. As a result of separation from the Highest, the primary concept "I am" arose and subsequently other concepts developed. Separation means otherness, duality.

V: I thought I heard you say that there is total non-differentiation at the supreme level. On that supreme level is there also total "I-am-ness"?

M: Out of "non-knowingness," knowingness appears: this knowingness should realize itself. When we speak, we should investigate from where the language arises. It sprouts from the sense of "I-am-ness," but what is the source of this "I-am-ness"?

Actually I do not talk; only when occurring spontaneously does the talk express itself. But the primary occurrence is the reminder "I am," out of which springs the language and the talk. So, what is this "I-am-ness"?

Remember that in the primary reminder "I am" the whole cosmos and your body exist. All bodies are created from and sustained on material (biological) essences, but the sense of being is the quintessence, *sattva-guna*, of the body. Who and from where is this sense of being? This has to be thoroughly investigated. When this is done, while abiding necessarily in the knowledge "I am"—the sense of beingness—an amazing revelation will be made, namely that from your own seed-beingness the whole manifest universe is projected, including your body. This supreme and powerful principle, though being itself without a form and name, upon sensing "I am" instantly embraces the body and mistakenly accepts this as its own. It clings to the body-identity so quickly that the fact of its own independent existence is easily missed.

The essence of being, which is humming "I am," is a prerequisite for any functioning of the body. When a person is sick and there is no response when the patient is called or beckoned, this sense of being is clouded.

V: Should one fall asleep as many times as possible in order to experience "I-am-ness" in the waking state?

M: "I-am-ness" cannot be experienced or recognized from the body-mind sense. It is the "I-am-ness" that makes the body and senses function and experience.

You are quite knowledgeable; now understand this: if you think you are dying, it shows you still identify with your body and that your knowledge "I am" has not merged in itself, which also indicates that you have not attained *jnana-yoga*.

Your spiritual knowledge, therefore, smacks of impurity. While you are actually the manifest knowledge "I am," you cling to a body as yourself. This is the impurity. We talked about death, which is the end point of life; but what about the starting point, the birth? Prior to birth you were in the womb for nine months. During that period, did you have *humkara* — the humming of beingness? Immediately after birth, the indwelling beingness does not yet feel itself palpably. After a few months, recognition starts. Still later the child begins to know various objects, such as his body and his mother, as also sounds and words. At this stage, through the mother, he knows his name and other ideas.

You as a fetus, did you know yourself in the womb of the mother?

V: But there was no consciousness in that form.

M: Was it knowing itself in those nine months in the womb?

V: No, but it was there.

M: Consciousness is all-prevailing, but it remained dormant in the fetus because it was not a fully developed body.

V: But it was in the fetus.

M: Where is the argument? Consciousness is everywhere, it is in the flowers, you, me, everywhere!

V: Good, good, I have understood.

M: What did you understand?

V: That there is nothing else but consciousness.

M: No, this is not it. The correct understanding will be when you realize that whatever you have understood so far, is invalid. With the fulfillment of *jnana-yoga*, all that which is understood is made unreal.

The so-called sages who revel in powers obtained, and in the honor received as a result, are not fully realized because their abidance in the Self is not complete. A child, who was unblemished, is fed with ideas, just as the blank screen of a T.V. set displays pictures transmitted from the outside. The child principle, which is consciousness, is the product of a "chemical process." I like to refer to consciousness as "chemical." But You, at the highest level, are not that chemical in which all the world drama happens. Suppose you are a hundred-year-old who holds on to this memory that he is a hundred years old. It is the chemical. For example, look at the picture of my guru on the wall here. Now who is holding on to the image of my guru? It is the "chemical" of the photograph.

Now this "chemical" in the body holds on to an identity and carries out activities through the body. I call this expression "mechanical."

V: But the "chemical" photograph could not have retained the picture of your guru if he had not been there.

M: But who is this guru and where would this memory "I am" as well as the "chemical" be if the Highest, that is the Absolute, was not there? The eternal existence of the Absolute alone makes the appearance of consciousness and all world-play possible, so the world-play is an image created by consciousness.

V: Has universal consciousness taken the form of Maharaj?

M: That speck of consciousness has taken the form of universal consciousness. Its image is the entire universe, just like the pinprick of consciousness in deep sleep develops into a dream-world.

V: Does it mean that you are in my dream-world?

M: Before referring to "me" as "you," investigate as to what "you" are. Just as a boomerang hits the person who throws it, similarly your own question has bounced back on you, so "you"—what is that? And what is more, I am not the body, nor that "chemical" even.

This "chemical" or the consciousness is also called *maha-tattva*, *moolamaya*, *hiranyagarbha*, *brahma-sutra* etc....but the sum total of all this is the *atma-prem*, the love of the Self. The one who understands and realizes the *maha-tattva* is called the "Mahatma." Presumptuously, you may think you are a *jnani*, but if you think so you are an ignorant person only.

V: So the Awareness is the highest possible term used. Awareness appears to be above "I-am-ness."

M: Yes, provided Awareness does not feel "I-am-ness." The knowledge of the entire universe merges into that highest state. Whatever qualitative manifestation is there, it is called *Bhagavan*. All the titles and statuses suggested by the titles, and everything else, have merged into Nothingness. The Ishwara which has become the *visvavishaya*—that is, the universal manifestation—has become *nirvishaya*—that is, one without the subjectivity even. This can be understood only by those who are extremely keen to know their own nature. Whatever information I give is about that spark, the speck of consciousness, which has delivered this manifest universe. Further, I the Absolute am not that speck. But I cannot give any information about Me, the Absolute. There have been so many dissolutions of cosmoses and universes, so also aeons have come and gone, but I the Absolute remain untouched, and my kingdom is ever quiet. Suppose a question is asked of you, what were you a hundred years back? You would reply "I was not." That means, I was not like "this," that is, like this present "I am." Who (and how) could (he) say "I was not like this"? The one who says this, was he not there? The one who was prior to a hundred years was not like this present "I am" but he was and is now.

V: He is this "I," the Absolute.

M: All right, use whatever words and concepts you like and satisfy yourself. When I call someone a "cheat," it satisfies me, and also I call someone a "Mahatma" because it satisfies me. What were you a hundred years ago? Ponder over it.

Why do you not investigate the point of conception and its further development? Instead, you are too busy acquiring spiritual and worldly gains. That will not help.

In the vegetable juices and food essences this *svarasa*, sense of knowingness, and *prarabdha*, destiny, exist already in dormant condition. And the quintessence of the food essences and juices is the sense of being or the knowledge "I am."

V: But could that principle be there without *prana*?

M: Who should be there without *prana*?

V: Is it in the flower?

M: Not only in flowers but even in the color. It is every-where. After listening to the knowledge that I am expound-ing, what will happen? One who understands and imbibes the knowledge will come to the conclusion that whatever is seen, heard, experienced and acquired is totally useless and redundant. Finally, no one will remain but the *nishkama Parabrahman*, the desireless eternal Absolute state. We go on with spiritual disciplines such as worshipping a God, penance, *japa* etc. to acquire something spiritual. And if the purpose is attained, it will be *nishkama Parabrahman*, which proves everything is useless. Even the highest is useless to the highest. This state is also titled *Poorna-brahman*, *Para-matman*, and *Parameshvara*. Now go back one day prior to your conception. That is also the *Poorna-brahman* state; there was no need for anything then.

V: I try to follow my thoughts and feelings, but I find that they are changing all the time. I know this changing happens against a background of the changeless in me. Will this way of thinking be useful to me?

M: Yes, it will be useful but...Intellectually it is all right, but the thinking is unreal. What do you mean by the changeless? When could there be the changeless? Only when you do not know "you are"...when the sense of being totally merges in itself. Were you not in that changeless state, a day prior to your conception? From your body-mind sense you observe everything as separate entities, such as "I," "you," "we," "they," etc. But to the changeless Absolute all this play of cosmos and universe happens in the cell of beingness. Which identity has remained unchanged from childhood to your present age? No identity in the world can ever remain the same and unchanging!

V: I think the "I principle" does not change, is it not so?

M: Your "I principle" has still not understood. It is the product of the five-elemental play, which is always in a state of flux. So how can you attribute the quality of "I-am-ness" to the Absolute state? In that state there is no scope at all for any play of the five elements! It is a state without any attributes.

Suppose the Absolute had a little sense of this "I-amness," would it care to enter a womb?

V: During my meditation, attention is on consciousness itself. I realize I am aware of that pure consciousness and so I am not it.

M: Your spiritual background is good. You talk about pure consciousness which is all-pervading manifestation and functioning. And in this state witnessing happens. The fulfillment of meditation rests in totally obliterating the memory and non-memory of manifestation along with the sense of being. So long as the *guna*, sense of being, is there, witnessing happens. Abidance in the non-witnessing state is the *advaita* state, the highest; therefore, all experience must be swallowed, including the feeling of the sense of being, which is the primordial experience.

V: As I have said earlier, when I am aware of that pure consciousness, at that point I am quite independent of my body and circumstances. I feel myself, the Absolute, as the origin of that consciousness. And behind this consciousness, the "I" as Absolute remains in silent repose.

M: You are talking of consciousness, now tell me: What is the cause of this consciousness? It is the result of what, the product of what?

SECOND VISITOR: Consciousness is a product of food.

M: Yes, in the food essence, in this quality or *guna*, the sense of "I-am-ness" dwells. But understand clearly, you or I are not that *guna* from the Absolute standpoint. We, the Absolute, are only posing as "I-am-ness"; as the Absolute, we are not that chemical "I am."

FIRST VISITOR: Later in my meditation I seem to move away from my state of awareness of pure consciousness and slide back into bodily and mental existence. I seek your help at this point.

M: Do nothing, absolutely nothing! Just be, be the knowledge "I am" only and abide there.

To imbibe this, meditate on beingness only. Catch hold of the knowledge "I am" in meditation. In this process, the realization occurs that "I" the Absolute am not the *guna* "I am"; therefore, in meditation nothing is to be retained as memory. Nevertheless, something will appear on the memory screen, but be unconcerned; just *be*, do nothing. Refrain from grasping anything in meditation; the moment you do, otherness begins, and so duality. Nothing is to be done. Then all your riddles will be solved and dissolved. *Moolamaya*—that is, the primary illusion—will release her stronghold on you and will get lost.

In spirituality there is no profit or loss, so also there will be no question of birth and death. As a matter of fact, you have no direct experience of birth! It is something like the incident of robbery that happened in Calcutta and of which I, residing in Bombay and never having been to Calcutta, am accused. Similarly, I am charged, not only with this birth but also hundreds of previous births. I am not aware of any birth; only my "parents," whom I never knew, are charging me with this birth.

With this state of affairs, are you not ashamed of accepting the "charge" of your birth? I was absolved of all these imaginary charges, when I met my *sat-guru*, who lit the torch of wisdom and showed me my true nature as the Unborn. In the domain of the Unborn there is no place for the "I am" nor for the sun, the moon, the stars, the cosmos etc.

February 10th 1980

12.

WHATEVER IS PERCEIVED, YOU ARE NOT

ISITOR: I have read *I Am That* and came here on my own.

MAHARAJ: Have you read the whole book?

V: I have read the first part fully and the second partially.

M: Having read the book, did you come to your self at the witnessing state?

V: Yes, I understood but I do not feel it. I have no peace of mind.

M: Do you get an inkling as to how you are connected with your self?

V: A little bit.

M: Would you like to ask any questions?

V: Not many, but I shall be grateful if I am told how to bring peace to my mind.

M: Because of the self, the *atman*, you are connected to the world through the body. The self is nothing else but the knowledge that "you are." Meditate on that principle by which you know "you are" and on account of which you experience the world. Meditate on this knowledge "you are," which is the consciousness, and abide therein.

V: But the concentration is just not there.

M: Ignore the mind the way you disregard the crowd you encounter on the streets.

V: I shall try.

M: As a matter of fact, mind is a universal dynamic principle, but we restrict it to the limits of the body and then depend on it—hence all the trouble. Consider the water in Lake Tansa. That water belongs to the whole of Bombay. Out of that water, can we claim some as yours or mine? In a similar vein, understand that the self is universal. But you have conditioned it by confining it to the body; therefore, you face problems. This self is also termed Ishwara—God—the Universal Principle. If you hold on to that, profound knowledge will descend upon you and you will have peace.

V: I try to meditate on that, but the mind wanders here and there. If I try to remain indifferent to mind, it will be a long-drawn-out process.

M: But are you not the root of any process?

V: The root of everything is life.

M: Yes, but the life force is universal and not personalized. Once you realize this, you have no more troubles.

V: That is right, but when the mind goes astray I have trouble. Sometimes I feel that life is universal, but at moments it becomes individualized. How to get rid of this?

M: This is the conventional way of talking. The water is universal, use it when you possess it. Similarly, use the mind to meet your needs and then let it flow by itself without your interference and involvement, like the flow of a river from where you take water only when needed.

My talks are meant for intelligent people. [*To a local visitor:*] Why have you come? You will not understand these talks; you only sing *bhajans* in praise of God.

Why do I respect those foreign visitors? They are earnest seekers, in search of Truth, but they have not been able to locate it. I appreciate their sincerity and deep urge to understand.

V: They really go far. Any subject they take, they explore deeply into it.

M: Although the two of us talk here, in actuality they (the two entities) are not there. This is the theme today. At first, "no one" is. Instantly, one is, and then two. The subject of the talk is: How did these two reduce to one, and finally to nothing? Out of nothingness spontaneously the sense of beingness is felt—this is one. Later, when the sense of beingness knows "I am," duality begins. Then, after the duality has arisen, the sense of beingness identifies with the form, and so on. Actually to refer to the sense of being as "one," is not quite correct. Since in this state only the sense of being prevails, where is the need to say even "one"? With the appearance of otherness (duality), both no. 1 and no. 2 appear simultaneously. To say, "something is," "I" must be there first. If "I" am not, I cannot say "something is." So the fundamental principle in spirituality is that "I" must be there, before anything else can be. This "I" is the beingness which is first.

V: You said, in the beginning there is "one," and later there is "none."

M: When one looks into one's self, that is, when one abides in the self, then there is "none."

V: Yet, when one merges, one remains.

M: To say that, is all right in common parlance, but actually it is nothing of the sort.

V: But you said that life is eternal, so life is there.

M: But not the life of an individual; it is the Absolute transcending the universal consciousness.

V: Life is eternal, that means life is there for ever.

M: Yes, life potential is always there. But unless a body-form is available, there cannot be any sense of perception. When the body drops dead, the senses do not function; therefore, no perception or knowing of the world takes place for that entity.

Only so long as the senses operate is perception and knowing of the world possible. So, in a way, the absence of sensory function is liberation. Isn't that correct?

At present, I am alive and my senses and reflexes react to situations. The senses and reflexes of a dead person do not react. In the manifested universe, when the capacity for sensory perception and motor function is created in a body form, only then is existence of a perceptible universe possible. The main point is that for a universe to exist, there must be an observer with sense organs in proper working order. The mind interprets the sense perceptions and concludes that the universe exists. Therefore, if the observer's sense organs and mind do not operate, then the observer's universe does not exist.

V: But the senses of seeing, hearing and touching etc. belong to the body and not to the self, the *atman*.

M: Without *atman*, the senses cannot function. But it resides in the quintessence of the body. When it subsides in itself, only *nirguna* remains—the non-qualitative Absolute.

V: The *atman* can change bodies.

M: The *atman* has no body, so how can it change? At present, it presumes that "I am" means body only.

V: In this materialistic world, when we say "we" we mean the body only. But if my legs are removed, they are apart from me. Therefore, I feel that I as such am not the body.

M: That is correct.

V: So *atman* is something other than body.

M: *Atman* is not the individual, this must be firmly grasped. *Atman* feels the sense of being only through a body with senses operating, otherwise the *atman* does not feel itself.

V: To realize this, should I do meditation?

M: Yes, meditation is very necessary. If you can do it continuously, it is good, but with a daily occupation this is not always possible. Meditation done in the early morning hours is helpful and effective. But you may do it whenever you have leisure. Seekers with a deep urge can meditate at any time. In the beginning, a seeker should sit alone in a quiet spot with complete leisure at his disposal. When he attains stability in meditation, he can sit anywhere, anytime. Suppose such an advanced seeker sits here in meditation. He will be totally lost within himself. His attention will be focused on attention only, with the result that he will not be aware of what is going on around him. Further, in such a state nothing will occur to him. Meditation should be of this quality. Suppose somebody is deeply worried, would he take note of things going around him?

When you sit in deep meditation, your sense of being is totally infused with the knowledge "I am" only. In such a state it will be revealed to you intuitively as to how and why your sense of "I-am-ness" emerged.

V: By the "I-am-ness"?

M: Consciousness, beingness, sense of being, "I-am-ness," all are the same in you, prior to emanation of any words.

This is a subtle point, so try to understand it clearly. When I say "I was not" prior to conception, then what I actually mean is that I was not like this present "I am." But that "I" which could discern this must be there to judge the absence of the present "I am."

Owing to the absence of a body, that "I" prior to conception had no sense of being or sense of "I-am-ness." With the arrival of a body the sense of "I-am-ness" is imposed on the prior "I."

In meditation, this sense of "I-am-ness" only will indicate how and why it came about. You must be possessed by this idea of finding out what this "I-am-ness" is, just as you would not rest until you found the source of a smell emanating from some place. For example, if a foul smell emanates you will have to go to that source; and when you discover that it is the decomposed body of a rat, you will have to dispose of that body in order to get rid of the stink. Similarly, if a nice fragrance wafts in your direction, you would like to locate the flower. You must go to the source of this "I-am-ness" fragrance, and find out its "how and why."

V: How does one chase that?

M: The principle that gives rise to this "I-am-ness" fragrance is termed *Bhagavan-vasudeva*—the god who gives fragrance. The one who receives this fragrance wants to retain it at all costs.

V: How can one enter that state?

M: You, from the body-mind level, are incapable of tracking it down. But that principle alone will discover itself. Somebody you may call Bhagavan, or Vittal or God, is so infatuated with this fragrance that he wants to perpetuate it.

V: One day my efforts will bear fruit and I shall find him out automatically.

M: His significance for you will be nullified the moment he is discovered, and you will be liberated from that infatuation with *vasudeva*.

V: In other words, I think when you always feel it so, you don't go after it. Once you realize the self then it automatically comes to you, so there is no need for you to track it down. So once we realize it, we can use it the way we want.

M: In that state you will be beyond any needs and wants; you will have no use for anything. No desires will be left, because they are all fulfilled.

V: I did not mean that I should use it for my worldly needs. What I meant was that I would become one with it.

M: In actuality you were never detached from it. So where is the question of being one with it?

V: It is nice that I never got detached from it, but in my present state I consider myself only the body.

M: This is your concept, that you are the body, and it is deluding you.

V: Then I will be free.

M: [*Reciting a couplet of Guru Nanak:*]

O mind, what are you searching? Inside and outside it is one only. It is the concept that makes you feel inside and outside. Once the earthen pot bearing the name Nanak is broken, by getting rid of the concept that I am the body, where is inside and outside? It is "I" only prevailing everywhere.

Nanak further says:

Like the fragrance in a flower, like an image in a mirror, this sense of "I-am-ness" is felt in the body. Therefore, give up your name Nanak and also your identity with the body.

Abide in the sense of "I-am-ness" and you shall be liberated.

V: When I try to track down the self it seems to me that it creates more selves.

M: But who is it that sees so many selves? One thought produces further thoughts. Who observes the first thought?

V: This is what I want to know.

M: Only you are the observer of the first thought. If the knower of the very first thought is not there, who will observe the other thoughts?

V: If the knower is not, there will also be no thoughts.

M: If you understand this, everything is over—you can go. To expound and propagate concepts is simple. But to drop all concepts is difficult and rare.

V: How do I remove thoughts and new concepts? If all concepts and thoughts are removed, will I become one with that?

M: Do not try to become anything. Do nothing! Without thinking on any of your words, remain quiet. Once a word sprouts it creates a meaning and then you ride on it. You follow the meanings of your words and claim that you are in search of your self. So be wakeful to that state which is prior to the sprouting of words. Did you associate with any sages?

V: This is the first time.

M: Have you been reading any books?

V: I have been reading Paul Brunton's work on Ramana Maharshi.

M: Your spiritual background is ready, that is why you listen to the talks and try to understand them. Other people quarrel with me with their concepts. They are brimming over with concepts, with the result that they are unable to listen to what I say. Many people come here, presuming themselves to be very knowledgeable but I know that they are ignorant only. However, I consider them as consciousness alone.

All your identities at the body-mind level have been changing continuously, and none of them has been constant and faithful to you. Why then are you attracted to any of such identities by stating "I am like this," "I am like that"?

V: This is all mental. At certain moments I think I am "like this," at other moments I think I am "like that."

M: Who other than you is observing those moments? You are the witness of these moments. Whatever is seen and perceived and also whatever you see inside and outside you, that you are not.

V: I am trying to understand.

M: In meditation, you might convince yourself "I am Guru Nanak only," or as some people in their meditation firmly believe: "I am Bhagavan Sri Krishna only." None of such identities has any stability. The only stable one is the observer of those identities, and you alone are that observer—the eternal one.

Take the example of a poor actor who played the role of a king so splendidly that he received a lot of praise. But he is not the King. Similarly, you are not Guru Nanak. You are the observer. Whatever you see and perceive is all the play of *maya*, the illusive principle.

February 19th 1980

13.

YOU MUST EXIST PRIOR TO WITNESSING FOR WITNESSING TO HAPPEN

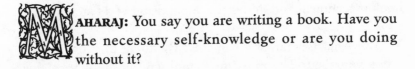**AHARAJ:** You say you are writing a book. Have you the necessary self-knowledge or are you doing without it?

VISITOR: I am not writing a book on self-knowledge.

M: If there is no self-knowledge, who then is the writer?

V: I am writing a book on yogic *asanas* in conjunction with a teacher. It was not something out of my own mind.

M: That is all right. But what about yourself, your nature, identity? You are writing something about physical activities.

V: Ultimately, yes, I would like to know myself.

M: If you are not, what else could there be? Why are you writing about these disciplines? It is only to know oneself, is it not?

V: This will prepare a background for the seeker, to prepare him for his search of the Self.

M: But is your own background ready?

V: No, of course not!

M: Then, why did you write the book?

V: Because it is a technical one, with pictures.

M: But the author does not know himself, so what's the use of the writings?

V: In that case I would rather be with you but, as I said, the book is technical and under the supervision of a teacher.

M: But what is your profit in this? By doing this job, do you attain your Self? The most important gain in life is to realize one's Self.

V: I agree with you. In a sense, I probably gained during the time I was working on the book, meaning that I have grown in experience and maturity.

M: That means with your experience you must have collected more concepts. Are you the one that grows in height and breadth?

V: No.

M: What is the purpose of your visit?

V: Every time I visit you, I have a feeling of inspiration and exaltation.

M: What is the use of that also?

V: I understand what you are driving at.

M: Who observes all this inspiration and exaltation? Who is the knower? You are not looking towards yourself, instead you are occupied with other things.

V: Do you mean to say that while looking into myself I should pursue my vocation also?

M: Once you look inwards, everything will follow spontaneously for you. Before you recognized your mother, all things that concerned you were happening spontaneously without your knowledge.

V: Yes, I agree.

M: You have developed into a human being naturally. Before this appearance, did you have any knowledge? Instead of paying attention to this aspect, you involve yourself in the affairs of others!

V: Shall I stop then with my present occupation?

M: There is no question of continuing or discontinuing your occupation. You should get to know yourself.

V: But what should I do until I see myself?

M: You have been doing something ...

V: Earlier you said, why was I involving myself in activities ...

M: Do not bother about doing or not doing; it is most important that you look at yourself.

SECOND VISITOR: But at least, he was doing something useful like writing a book on yoga.

M: What is yoga, what is that "linking"? Who meets what?

V: Union of the soul with God.

M: God is a word you have heard, while the soul is the direct experience of one's existence.

V: I just expressed the meaning of yoga as generally understood.

M: That means you do not understand true yoga. Do you know that only self-realized sages are worshipped, and not the yogis?

V: Am I wrong in following yoga?

M: Many *rishis* and ascetics have practiced yoga; but are they worshipped?
[*Addressing a newly arrived visitor, who had met Ananda Mayi Ma*] Did you attain the state of *ananda* when you went to her? If you had realized *ananda mayi*, you would never have visited her again nor would you have come here. If you understand what I say, that is more than enough.

V: It is not difficult to understand.

M: Then why do you sit here?

V: I would like to sit here for some time.

M: Since you have been to Ananda Mayi, let us know what *ananda* is. Does *ananda*—the Bliss—have a tangible form?

V: I do not think so. But one can feel happiness.

M: Agreed, but do you see it, can you observe it?

V: Sometimes, I can see the essence of happiness emanating from Ananda Mayi Ma.

M: Do you not think a knower has to be present prior to any seeing or feeling?

V: After reading *I Am That* I understand that a knower must be there before anything can be seen, felt or experienced.

M: You, as the witness, are prior to happiness. But the ultimate you, the real you, are prior to the witness-you. Happiness is not lasting.

V: Initially, during my meditation, when I had the experience of the "witness" within me, I was terribly afraid, because I felt that I was split into two; this I do not have any more.

M: You felt the split. Now which one was "you," the concept of "seeing," or the witness of the concept?

V: I did not have such clarity.

M: At least, talk from the intellectual level, if you did not directly experience the subtlety.

V: I am the observer of the split.

M: Explain the two stages.

V: I was afraid that I would see the splitting.

M: Was it the splitting of the concept or was it the splitting of yourself?

V: Neither.

M: Yes, You, the Absolute, are neither one nor two. But you are prior to both.

In the earlier days in India, when the head of the country rode in his car, its license plate had no number. Similarly, you do not need a number, being the Highest. [*Maharaj is again talking to the visitor who wrote books on yoga*] You are a yogi, and so you understand what I am saying.

V: Yes, I understand a little but I am not a yogi.

M: But you have been studying yoga systems and practicing yoga. When you throw sugar or salt into water, they dissolve in it. Now I ask you in what did you merge?

V: Sometimes I merge.

M: At other times?

V: I was reciting the sacred name, doing *japa*.

M: The purpose of *japa* is to conserve oneself, that means the knowingness is to be retained. *Japa* in Marathi means to guard, to protect. You should protect your beingness by *japa*.

ANOTHER VISITOR: What is beingness?

M: What "you are," the knowledge that "you are," without words, just the sense of beingness. Who went to Ananda Mayi Ma, the body or the beingness? The latter is prior to body, mind and eruption of any words. Did you practice *japa*?

V: Yes.

M: *Japa* is like a treatment given to your beingness, just as you take medicine and apply poultices to your body for its well-being.

V: That is what I feel strongly.

M: You feel relaxed.

V: Yes, very much, but now that I know something about witnessing I wonder how I would be doing *japa*.

M: Nevertheless, at the time you knew that you were doing *japa*.

V: Yes.

M: Then is this not witnessing or happening of witnessing to you?

V: Yes.

M: Witnessing happens naturally. When your words enter in me, I respond. Similarly, when we perceive anything through our senses, witnessing of the perceptions happens. No special efforts are called for.

V: I want to ask about meditation and yoga.
   Ten years ago Ananda Mayi Ma asked me to do *japa*. After some time I started witnessing the *japa* going on in me. Then Ananda Mayi Ma told me to pursue it. My problem is, how to attain "I-am-ness" and beingness.

M: The first witnessing is that "you are"; after that, all other witnessings occur.
   Unless the primary witnessing of "you are" happens first, any further witnessings are not possible. When the flow of words emanates in you, as I have already said, the witnessing of them happens naturally in you. I repeat once again: The sense that "you are" should appear first and, subsequently, the

flow of words and its witnessing take place simultaneously.
Therefore, are you not prior to words?

V: I do not know.

M: That is exactly the ignorance, and to recognize it is knowledge. In the final analysis, you, the Absolute, are not this knowledge.

V: May I ask a question?

M: Remember Ananda Mayi, and with this in mind put your question because she is your guru.

V: Now I feel I am alone and that there is no guru.

M: What you say is correct. In that understanding and only in that, you should stabilize. But before you came to this conclusion, did you understand what you are and what the guru is?

V: The guru is someone who tells me what to do and I obey what is told to me.

M: Shall we call the knowledge "I am" the guru?

V: Yes.

M: But even that "knowledge," you are not!

V: When you say "knowledge," do you mean consciousness?

M: Of course, "knowledge," "I am," means consciousness, God, Ishwara, guru etc., but You, the Absolute, are not that.

ANOTHER VISITOR: May I ask, who am I?

M: Are you there before asking or after?

V: Both ways.

M: This is to be understood and realized, that "I am" is even before the arising of any words and questions in me. People always want a name or concept to indicate the state of "I am" prior to words. When this is done by giving it a name, like for example Brahman, they feel satisfied.

V: I am not happy, I am very afraid.

M: Also right now, or previously?

V: Even now.

M: That fear is due to your identification with the body-mind. When you have no knowledge of the body, can there be fear?

V: No, when my guru told me I was the Brahman, this fear started.

M: Exactly, with those words of the guru, your body-mind had a shock because its dissolution began! The fear that you have is in the mind.

V: I know that, but I still have it. The body is afraid to be no more.

M: Coming back to Ananda Mayi Ma. When Ananda Mayi merges into *ananda mayi* (her Self), that is the Highest, the Absolute only. Ananda Mayi denotes a blissful state but still qualitative. It is consciousness.

V: Is *ananda mayi* of this world?

M: It is the other way, all the worlds rest in her womb. What is *ananda mayi*? Your state of bliss only, the knowledge "you are." If this is not, nothing is! You consider *ananda mayi* as a personality, but it is nothing of the sort. *Ananda mayi* is the state of Being.

March 13th 1980

14.

SUBTLER THAN SPACE IS THE SENSE OF "I-AM-NESS"

MAHARAJ: Beingness can act in the world only with the aid of a body. This body is the quintessence of the five elements, and the quintessence of the body-essence is the knowledge "I am." In the absence of a body form, the beingness cannot know itself. So, you should hold on to that indwelling principle, the beingness, only. The potential for all activities rests with beingness, which is in dormant condition in food-body juices. These juices emanate from the five elements. The presiding principle of the whole functioning is the knowledge "I am," which is the quintessence of the five-elemental body. This knowledge "I am" has to be understood correctly. The beingness, vital breath and mind are formless. In the course of the five-elemental flow, various body forms of the multifarious species are created. When the vital breath infuses these different body forms, the beingness also expresses itself through them. Vegetable essence, which is called *sattva*, goes into the making of the diverse bodies of species. And in the bodies dwells the *sattva* sense of being. Each species is given a name according to the shape or form of the body. Expressions and actions of the species vary according to their body forms.

Of all the species, the most evolved is the human being, who therefore qualifies for the title Ishwara, God. With the

functioning of the vital breath, mind flow begins in a human
body; and actions are performed according to *samskaras*,[1]
which are impressions collected from the outside by mind.

A body may be dark, fair, tall or short, but the indwelling
principle—which is the knowledge "I am"—has no color or
dimension, just like the vital breath and mind. It is merely a
"sense of presence," a feeling of effulgence. And mind functions like its vehicle or medium for executing worldly activities.

You want to meditate and so you should. Real meditation
is to abide in this sense of being. In fact, meditation means
the sense of being holding on to itself. It is said that after
death one goes to heaven or hell. But this is mere concept
and hearsay. When a body has died, the indwelling *atman*,
sense of being, loses memory of its beingness and does not
know "it is." In that state there is no sleep, waking and knowingness.

You should understand this clearly. If one thinks one is the
body, one becomes a slave of mind and suffers accordingly.
Therefore, you should completely identify yourself with the
highest principle in you, which is the knowledge "I am." This
will elevate you to the status of *brihaspati*—the guru of gods.

You think you are somebody; but you are nothing of the
sort. The sense of being is expressed through the body as a
consequence of the all-pervading Absolute. This sense of
being is deeply infatuated with itself and is termed *atma-
prem*, Self-love. It is also called *guna*, Shiva, and Brahman. It
is the Self-love that is functioning through different bodies.
Since there is only this principle expressing itself, in different
ways, through the different vehicles, there is no "you," "I," or
"he." When the body dies, it decomposes into the five primary elements; and the vital breath, *prana*, merges in the universal air. And the *guna*—that is, the sense of being—instantly
becomes *nirguna* or non-being, just as a flame is extinguished

1 A Western term that may be close to the Sanskrit meaning is 'engrams.'

instantly. Please listen to my talks intently.

If there is no vital breath, the *guna* has no quality of being. Only so long as the *guna* exists, do grand titles such as Shiva, Brahma, and Vishnu apply. Without *prana*, the vital breath, there is no movement or dynamic quality either of the body or even of the *guna*. In short, when its dear friend and attendant, *prana*, quits a body, the presiding principle, *guna*, also evaporates. In a heap of grain, consciousness is latent, and in the presence of favorable conditions, it will manifest according to the form and quality of the species. If you have any questions on this topic, please ask.

VISITOR: Are biological forms created naturally, without any purpose?

M: Yes, but a particular species procreates only within the pattern of its own image. Man does not beget a lower animal or vice versa. Coming back to the sense of "I-am-ness," you should understand that it is the subtlest principle, subtler than space even. When it is extinguished because of death of the body and stopping of the vital breath, the event is termed *niryana* or *nirvana*. This is a state in which there is no sample left of "I-am-ness"—a sampleless condition absolutely. The state does not know "it is" and is beyond happiness and suffering, and altogether beyond words; it is called the *Parabrahman*—a non-experiential state.

V: What is the blissful state in meditation?

M: When the meditator forgets himself totally in meditation; it is *vishranti*, which means complete relaxation ending in total forgetfulness. This is the blissful state, where there is no need for words, concepts or even the sense of "I am."

V: All concepts in us sprout out of the principle which was latent in the fetus. Is it not so?

M: Yes.

V: Could it be that our thought-emanation also is already decided?

M: The thoughts are not predestined but are the reactions of impressions, *samskaras*, which you receive now.

V: God or Ishwara is said to be omniscient—all-knowledgeable. What does that mean?

M: Ishwara is not an individual person. It is an all-pervading principle, which is latent in everything. It is manifest in the five elements, the three *gunas*, and in the cycle of waking, sleep and knowingness.

V: Does it mean no duality?

M: Duality is only at the body-mind level. In the all-pervading universal consciousness, millions of births take place every day, but in its basic Absoluteness it is *ajanma*—the Unborn. Although as universal consciousness it is multi-qualitative, as the Absolute state it is *nirguna*, non-qualitative.

[*To an American woman, who is a writer:*] You'd better go home soon, before you fully imbibe this knowledge; otherwise, you will be lost to all your "identities."

V: I cannot say ...

M: But I say, you will be relieved of the "comings and goings" of all your concepts; even your sense of "I-am-ness" will be liquidated. In this country, for ages it has been accepted that a sacred name carries great spiritual potency if recited properly; it has no better substitute. Millions of persons in the world are personified by the names given to them, because a name has utility on the worldly level. When you are initiated into a spiritual discipline with a sacred name, it means that it represents your "ultimate true nature." Be one with the sacred name completely, then it will give you all the mystic knowledge necessary for your spiritual elevation. It will awaken you into your "eternal awareness." This is the mystic key-word of the Navanath-Sampradaya, the traditional order of the Nine Gurus. These gurus were neither cultured nor highly educated. According to one of the stories, a man sat on one of the highest branches of a tree, cutting the very branch he sat on from the wrong side! A guru passing that way, seeing the naive man's one-pointed attention, took pity on him and blessed him with a name which the man recited diligently. In due course, this simpleton himself became a great sage. Such is the power of the sacred name recited with concentrated attention.

March 29th 1980

15.

MERGING OF BEINGNESS WITHIN ITSELF IS THE VERY FOUNT OF BLISS

MAHARAJ: Before the emanation of any words, "I" already exist; later I say mentally "I am." The word-free and thought-free state is the *atman*.

The *atman* per se is self-sufficient. But when it clings to the body, "treatments" such as mental and physical recreation or occupation are necessary; without these the *atman* cannot be tolerated by a person. For spiritual evolution, which is a requisite in the disengagement of the *atman* from body-identity, various disciplines have been recommended. Amongst these, the best is *namasmarana*—recitation of a holy name of God. But here God means the indwelling principle within you—the *atman*, which is given various names. These represent this "inner-God" who will respond no matter what names of other Gods you chant. The custom of counting beads of a rosary is merely to give occupation to your hands, but it is this inner God that you are supposed to invoke. This God is awakened when you tell the beads by reciting his name. Just as the cow's udders ooze out milk upon the sight of its calf who runs to its mother mooing "ama-ama," so also the beingness showers grace on the one who chants its holy name and tells beads in all earnestness by leading him into quietude. The keynote of recitation is to confine this "I-am-ness" within itself. The listener in you listens to the chantings and feels greatly pleased. This is the reason that people used to the daily chantings and telling of beads get restless when unable to do so.

Tukaram, the poet-saint of Maharashtra, affirms this same principle, when he sings in one of his couplets:

> Triumphant am I, in locking in my beingness
> in itself, with my devotion.
> Thus have I reached the very pinnacle of my
> spiritual search, resulting in the drying up of
> my mental inclinations.[1]

The merging of beingness within itself is the very fount of bliss. Many sages who are in such a state are quite oblivious of their physical condition and simply lie on the ground, revelling in themselves. Some misguided seekers, with the aid of drugs such as marijuana, artificially induce a state of forgetfulness. But this is benumbing the senses by extraneous means. Such people will not have enduring peace, only hangovers and sour heads. If you want eternal peace, you can have it and be it through the absorbing devotional path—the *nama-japa* or *bhakti-yoga*.

March 30th 1980

---

1 By "mental inclinations," Tukaram apparently refers to what in Hinduism is commonly called "latencies" or *vasanas*. These are the aggregate of latent desires (i.e., desires below the level of consciousness), innate tendencies and deeply ingrained habits which all give continuity to the pseudo-entity called "ego." Their obliteration must be seen as a necessary condition for Liberation. The exhaustion and eventual elimination of these psychological energies (that underlie the "mental modifications") is sometimes referred to by Indian sages as the "purification of the mind."

16.

TRY TO UNDERSTAND THE IGNORANT-CHILD PRINCIPLE

MAHARAJ: What I am talking about is the knowledge of totality. It is not a piece of information. I ponder over manifestation as a whole, while you pick up only a fragment, a concept out of my talks, and say "I like this idea" and then give it a high status by naming it as Brahma, Vishnu etc. But you do not attempt to comprehend the total and "wholesome" meaning.

VISITOR: You have been talking about this ignorant-child principle. Could you explain this a bit more fully?

M: When an infant is born, he is just an innocuous form of flesh and bones and all innocence. He has no mentation but has the instinct for eating, evacuation and crying. In due course, this lump of flesh develops the capacity for knowledge and action. Gradually, the knowingness "I am" is felt by it and this is followed by the mind. This "I-am-ness" feeling before the formation of mind is the ignorant-child principle, termed the *balkrishna* state. It is this very principle which is the source or foundation on which the infancy develops into childhood, boyhood, teenage and so on, undergoing physical and biological changes all the time. Eventually manhood is attained, when all physical and mental faculties reach their peak. But what is the root of all these attainments? It is that ignorant-child principle only, which developed with growth exclusively from inside to outside. During its growth to adulthood and later it receives, records and reacts to all the impressions through its senses and the mind. But all this happens only after it knows itself.

Your erroneous concept of knowledge is that of collecting information and ideas from the outside through the five senses of knowledge or perception. Then you give out this information to others as important knowledge and are fascinated by it. But when I talk about knowledge, I do not refer to this but to the knowledge that "you are," your beingness, to the child principle or the *balkrishna* state, which is the root cause of all your acquisitions, both spiritual and worldly. You should try to understand what this child principle is. I am dealing with this only and not with your so-called "knowledge" gained externally through the senses.

This *balkrishna* principle has great potential. It is the "chemical" that can develop photographic memories, can retain and reproduce whatever was read or heard only once. This is the innate capacity of the "non-knowing," ignorant-child principle, *balkrishna*. Here *bal* means the food essence, child-body, and *krishna* means "non-knowing," that is, ignorance. But it has the potential to receive, respond and react.

You are not doing anything. All this is happening spontaneously in you. If you want to understand the deep underlying meaning of this, go to the very source, to your beingness, and hold on to that. But above all, do not collect concepts.

Here, these talks proceed as automatically as breathing. Hundreds of people come and listen to the talks, but I do not assume any pose. Why? In the speck of my beingness, with the beingness, while I observed myself and everything else, realization occurred to me. Henceforth, all happenings took place spontaneously. Even the talks here are spontaneous occurrences, and so I am not the speaker. Nor am I, in this state, the child principle, *balkrishna*, as I abide in the Absolute.

April 4th 1980

17.

To Know What One Is, One Must Know One's Beginning

ISITOR: What is the difference between spirituality and discrimination?

MAHARAJ: Discrimination means selecting words and meanings worthy of us. Nevertheless, words that are worthy of our true nature and describe our ultimate state are never available.

Out of a heap of wheat, you pick up and collect good wheat for your consumption, while rejecting stones and bad wheat. Similarly, discrimination is to be used.

At present, you identify yourself with your body and mind. Therefore, in the initial stages of your spiritual practice, you should reject the identity by imbibing the principle that "I am" is the vital breath and the consciousness only and not the body and mind. In the later stages, the vital breath and the consciousness—that is, the knowledge "I am"— merge in one's ultimate nature, just as the thoughts of a professor or *pandit* subside in him when he goes to sleep. A person in deep sleep does not know himself, because even the sense of his beingness has merged in him.

When you realize that you are neither the body nor the mind, you will remain unaffected by any mental modifications. In that state, you are the dynamic universal consciousness. You should abide in this state.

Pleasure, pain and miseries are felt so long as identification with the body and mind is retained. Suppose a ship sank in mid-ocean with thousands of passengers. Could their identities survive the calamity in the absence of their bodies and minds? Further, could the victims have any idea about themselves after such a tragedy, when their bodies have totally vanished? Under these circumstances, even their surviving relatives are unable to visualize the state of the unfortunate passengers. To determine an identity, a body, vital breath, and the beingness are prerequisites.

V: Compassion, forgiveness, peace and attachment relate to the domain of human existence. Am I right in saying this?

M: These qualities are significant so long as the beingness is there, as a result of the functioning of a body and the vital breath. When these three principles function coherently, everything is there; otherwise nothing is.

Spirituality means abidance in the Self. When you discuss or think of any topic such as discrimination or spirituality, you study it objectively[1] and fractionally. But I do it subjectively[2] and totally by pointing to the all-embracing principle, the Self. Understand the Self; *be* the Self.

So long as your body, the vital breath and the beingness are there, you know that "you are." When the vital breath goes, the body drops off and the beingness extinguishes; the process is termed "death." One who is dead cannot know anything. A dead one does not know "he is," or "he was." So there is no registering of such a "dead" one's existence either with us or with the one.

Go to the root of your beingness. In the process, the

---

[1] and [2] From the dualistic standpoint of separate objects ("objectively"), in which the subject itself is one "object" among others, rather than from the standpoint of the Self, which is the totality and thus the ultimate Subject or Subjectivity ("subjectively").

beingness will be transcended and the ultimate "You" only remain, without the knowledge "you are."

That ultimate state is known as *vishranti*, which means total rest, complete relaxation, utter quietude etc.

The other meaning, by splitting the word, would be *vishara-anti*—forget yourself in the end. That means, in the ultimate state, "you-are-ness" is totally forgotten. Whether "I am" or "I am not," both are forgotten. This is the highest type of rest—*parama-vishranti*. Don't meekly accept what I say. If you have doubts, by all means ask questions. If anybody is going to ask questions, they will be from the body-mind level, and mind means whatever one has collected from the outside. It is not one's own. So, ask only about what has been discussed and from the correct standpoint.

V: How to experience that Highest State?

M: There is no question of experiencing. You are that state only.

V: All experience is derived through the senses.

M: Yes, but "You," the ultimate experiencer, are not merely the sum total of experiences.

On waking up, you know "you are"; this is your knowingness. Prior to this knowingness, whatever "you are," it is not the knowingness.

V: Does this have anything to do with the Ultimate?

M: There are many titles and attributes, but prior to all attributes, "You" are.

V: Do we have realization?

M: These are all concepts. The ultimate state, however, is beyond the grasp of words. Out of one concept more concepts are born, and everything is going on with and through these concepts. Thus, the storehouse is filled with concepts. But when the primary concept itself is abolished, where is the question of further concepts?

V: Is this "I" exaggerated or not?

M: What is your age?

V: Sixty-one years.

M: Going back in time to one day prior to those sixty-one odd years (of your life span), did you know that you were going to take birth?

V: Obviously not. I had no idea that I was going to be born, before my birth.

M: Now having been born, did you ever inquire why at all you were born? Earlier, this "I-am-ness" knowledge was not there before birth.

V: I do not know when I was born, nor do I know when I am going to die.

M: But all these days, why did you not make the inquiry? Now that you have the knowledge "I am," how did you come to it? Granted that you were born unknowingly, but like a man asleep on waking finds that he has a large boil, will he not inquire, "When did I get this boil?"

V: I did inquire.

M: With whom did you inquire? What answer did you get?

V: But I did not get any answer.

M: How and why this knowledge "I am"? That you must know. How did this knowledge "I am" appear from the "non-knowing" state?

V: I don't know.

M: You must know that. What is the use of all types of information? Thousands of people have drowned in a ship. What information can you have about their present state?

V: Death.

M: Obviously nothing. Can the one who did not know about death or birth have knowledge of his death?

V: We shall have to inquire from the dead person.

M: Are you going to inquire from the dead?
    Unknowingly this knowingness has appeared. How? From "Nothingness" this "I-am-ness" has appeared. How? Prior to your birth, did you ever experience your "I-am-ness"?

V: Probably not.

M: Why "probably"?

V: Definitely no. Collection of any information regarding the "non-knowing" state is merely an idle inquiry.

M: Why do you clasp that knowingness now, since you are going to meet death definitely? Prior to birth you did not know you were. You are going to die, then why are you clinging to all these concepts of heaven, hell, virtue and sin? Will you care to turn around and observe, now that you have heard all these talks?

V: Sometimes I do.

M: What is the use of that?

Finally, you must come to the conclusion that there is no such thing as the "me" and the "mine." See at least your beginning.

V: Probably we have a right to the beginning, and not to the end.

M: I am interested only in your beginning. How did you happen to be? It is most important.

V: I am interested in me and myself.

M: But did you come to know what you are?

V: You bless me.

M: You place before me your identity, then I will bless it. When one does not know his very beginning, how can he plead for anyone?

Although you know full well that you do not know, why do you still embrace all this?

V: It is instinct; we naturally embrace all this.

M: What is that instinctive uprising? What is it that is born? You are not concerned about it. You do not have that knowledge, because you do not have the urge. If you have a deep urge, then only will there be illumination. Until then you will be making all the efforts, while someone else will be taking the advantage, like a blind man working on a grinding stone while a dog eats all the flour.

V: How should we get rid of this blindness?

M: By abiding in the Self through insistence. Meditate on the Self. You must do the *hatha-yoga* of insistence and perseverance to have perfect knowledge about the Self.

V: Is there anybody who has such knowledge?

M: Yes, a rare one, one in ten million. Having come upon these mathematical odds, do you now give up on the inquiry?

V: I do not want to give up.

M: Have you come to this conclusion after pinching your ears?

V: What is the use of striving all along?

M: What is the use of any of your concepts? A *jnani* is beyond concept. He gives no importance to any concept.

V: He may not know how much we are striving now and have done so earlier; you have no idea. Ramakrishna Paramahamsa appealed to the Mother, "O Mother, take me beyond thought and knowledge, as I get mad with them."

M: Did you try it yourself, to go beyond thought and knowledge? If not, why do you refer to others?

V: No.

M: If you have not tried the recipe on yourself, why do you talk about it? Why do you introduce someone else's judgement? Can you remain alive without words? Without them, how can you manage your daily activities? I know the history of your birth. Why you call a person your "father" or "mother," I know full well. Why do you bother about others, instead of bothering about your own self—others such as Ramakrishna Paramahamsa? If you are ignorant, it is all right to inquire about others. But when you are concerned about yourself, then inquire about yourself only. When I pleased my "I-am-ness" by understanding it, only then did I come to know this "I-am-ness" and in the process also discovered that "I," the Absolute, am not that "I am." Stay put at one place. Having collected all the knowledge, ponder over it in seclusion.

V: If Maharaj blesses me, I shall have enlightenment.

M: That is not so simple. It is just like saying that a married couple will beget children merely if somebody blesses them.

V: The knowledge "I am" is a curse.

M: It is accidental, spontaneous. The beginning of "I am" is when I get the phone message that "I am." And when I have the information "I am," that is the *ganesha* state.

V: Why is *ganesha* equated with the primordial sound *pranava* that is "Om"?

M: Because *ganesha* represents the knowledge *prana*, the vital breath. Out of the *pranava*, the product of *prana*, the vocal language develops, after passing through four stages— that is, *para, pashyanti, madhyama* and *vaikhari. Para* is the source and the subtlest stage, while *vaikhari* is the grossest, representing the bursting out of vocal language. The state prior to *para* is "Love to be," the sense of love, which gives rise to all activities. That state is *ganesha*.

July 26th 1980

18.

Your Beingness Is the Beginning and End of the Mind

ISITOR: One Spanish gentleman, who visited here, had practiced a lot of meditation but he could not get rid of attachment.

MAHARAJ: So long as you are attached to the body, you will not be able to transcend attachment to various people and things.

V: Whenever I try to get hold of myself, I feel the absence of love for my relatives.

M: Do not be concerned about other people, be concerned with yourself.

V: After doing meditation, I lost love for others.

M: It is not that your love became less. The love now merges in your own self. Your own beingness is love and bliss. You have objectified your love.[1] Your very nature is love. By stabilizing in beingness you collect all the love which was diffused and spread outside. You abide in that knowledge "I

---

1 That is, through identification with "objects" (and this term includes "subjects"), the love which is infinite is inevitably made into a limited and relative thing.

151

am." Whatever "you are" inside the body represents love only. This love works, collects food, eats, digests, and acquires knowledge. "You are" is the love, and expresses itself through the vital breath; that is, activities go on because of the vital breath. Just as the body has a number of limbs for carrying out worldly activities, so the knowledge "you are" has the vital breath as its limb for activity. It is not a question of loving others, but directly knowing what "you are." That love is looking after you; it is your nourishment, your motive and energizing force. You focus your attention there. Its movement is indicated by the vital breath; it is the life force. The tangible feeling of its manifestation is the knowledge "you are." This love is the universal love. Not directed at any particular person or thing, it is very much like space. Space does not say, I am exclusively for so and so. It does not make love privately to someone. That love is manifest and universal. Because you identify with the body, all the troubles begin. Primary love is "love to be"; only after that can you think of loving others. Why do you strive "to be"? Simply, because you "love to be." The biggest stumbling block is the identification with the body-mind. Understand that it is not that you can become God; you *are* God. You are godly, originally, but you become something you are not. You should understand that your destination is your own self, the "I am." It is the very source of everything. That "I am" is to be realized.

V: That is the destination, but how to reach it?

M: You are derailed from the search because of the body. You toppled from the godly vantage point by catching hold of the body. Because "you are," the consciousness is. Before you say "I am," you already are.

V: Agreed.

M: You know now that "you are." Be that. Here I am not

going to tell you what is written in the scriptures, however sophisticated they may be. I am going to tell you simply that "you are." If you like my talks, you may come; if you do not like them, then stay away. At present, you may consider yourself to be an insignificant person of limited worth, intelligence. But actually it is not so. You are very ancient. You are infinite, eternal. This feeling of "I-am-ness" is like an advertisement; it indicates that eternal state. "I am"—the word or the "I am" feeling that you get inside you—is not eternal. But You are eternal and ancient.

V: How to understand that I am the eternal?

M: This cannot be understood in the usual intellectual way; that state is spontaneously realized. When you are in the state of "I-am-ness," you merge in the eternal state. Now you know that you are and that you are sitting. How did you develop this conviction?

V: I know I am sitting here.

M: In the same way, you must develop the conviction that you are the Absolute; this is most important. You have to focus your attention on that only. Before the appearance of the beingness or knowingness, I, the Absolute, am already there, eternally. Who will focus attention? Who knows that this is focusing of attention? That which focuses attention is prior to attention.

In the mind, how can you meditate? In what you call "meditation," you need an object. Who observes the meditation? Who practices the meditation? The process necessitates the presence of "someone" as well as an "object," does it not? But before anything else, the Meditator must be present. Now let Him alone be, without any object. In true meditation, the Meditator is "alone," without any object to meditate upon.

Prior to the waking state, I, or the Absolute, ever is. On waking it dawns upon me that "I am." And only after that, all other happenings and things come to mind. Again, I, the Absolute, must be before the waking state. Stay put here. Abide therein. You have to stabilize in your present true nature, "I am." All other secondary and redundant objects should be got rid of. Do not focus your attention on any of these things. The whole process is to be in your source. At present, what is your source? "I am." Catch hold of that "I-am-ness" and be in it.

You have to realize your own self. You must be at the borderline between "I am" and "Not-'I am'". Suppose it does not occur to you that "you are." Does it mean that you are not? If that "I-am-ness" is not there, You, the Absolute, are. As such, You prevail prior to, during and after the waking state. During the waking state the sense of your "I-am-ness" perceives the world; and from the standpoint of You, the Absolute, there is witnessing of your "I-am-ness" and its perceptions.

V: I want to do something spiritual.

M: Do you want self-knowledge or not? You want to do something spiritual, but you must be there for doing something. You must know "You." Who is the doer of spirituality? "I am" is the doer. When you are involved in daily activities, in the house, street and office, "who" is the common factor? It is your "I-am-ness." This "I-am-ness" of yours is doing everything.

Suppose from morning till night I have been doing a lot of things. What is the sum total of my activities? All these many activities took place in my state of beingness. In deep sleep, "I am" went into oblivion; it forgot itself. Then what is the use of everything that was done? Beingness is not an eternal state. It is a temporary phase—a passing show. Consciousness is the product of the five elements and their interactions. The result of the five elements is temporary, and time-bound. Your knowingness and all that you accumulate always come subsequent to your beingness. You can know something only when knowingness knows "it is." Your fall occurs when you try to identify something within the sphere of consciousness as "yourself." Your consciousness manifests the world. When you try to equate the body with yourself, the fall begins.

V: Who thinks I am the consciousness?

M: You! Without beingness, there is no thinking. Beingness is a basic precondition for thinking or not-thinking. Suppose you have pain in the body. Who witnesses that pain? Your beingness only witnesses it. In the absence of beingness, how can there be witnessing at all? The real witness is the eternal Self only. So long as beingness is there, you are the beingness. When the beingness is not, you are the Absolute. Everybody that comes here has to go. Similarly, the beingness which has come, must go.

July 28th 1980

19.

For a Realized One, the Whole Functioning in the World is a *Bhajan*

Visitor: What does Maharaj think of the materialization and dematerialization of physical objects, as demonstrated by Satya Sai Baba? However, I do not want to restrict this phenomenon to Satya Sai Baba.

Maharaj: It is just entertainment. Leave it alone. What "you are" and what "I am" are also concepts.

V: Without concepts, the world could not function.

M: The world is going on. Nevertheless, whatever has appeared in worldly life is only illusion. An event which has happened already (or whatever is gone), does it come back?

V: No one knows.

M: Similar things may happen, but they will never be identical.

V: Can you tell me about reincarnation?

M: According to one's firm conviction, the one who dies will have another dream, in which he will be reborn.

V: What is the apparent cause of rebirth? Is it due to past *karma*? And is there such a thing as *karma* at all?

M: *Karma* comprises your physical and mental activities. But actually they are happenings due to the three *gunas*: *sattva*, *rajas*, and *tamas*; that is, beingness, dynamic quality, and the claim of doership, respectively.

V: How does one get away from oneself? Most people seem to be stuck in patterns which are fetters of concepts.

M: Who says that?

V: My observation.

M: So long as you know "you are," it is always with you and it never leaves.

V: How should I be liberated from the concepts?

M: First, you must come to know what "you are."

V: Can you suggest some techniques?

M: They are *tantra*, mantra and *yantra*. *Tantra* is a technique, mantra is a fixed series of sacred words, and *yantra* is a machine for spiritual progress. You should understand and assimilate what I expound and advocate; then be yourself and let go.

V: I cannot easily translate into action whatever you tell me.

M: It is not that you should transform yourself. You have actually converted yourself into something other than yourself. Now you should reconvert yourself into your original self. Stabilize in yourself.

Because you want "to be," you occupy yourself with talking and all else. To sustain this "you are," you carry out various activities; thus, you keep your mind busy. But to the realized one, the mind-flow is like the release of obnoxious gases from below. The one who is stabilized in the self looks down upon the mind-chattering as though it were dirty and unwanted like those gases in the stomach.

When you are in the ignorant state, questions arise about good and bad and about making choices for accepting or rejecting. But in the state of knowledge, things happen spontaneously and there is no choosing and discarding. Even the apparently ritualistic actions of a realized one, such as *bhajans*, singing or chanting in praise of gods etc. are spontaneous expressions. They are not planned but just happen. For the realized one, the whole functioning in the world is a *bhajan*. All the happenings are the result of "you," the motive force. Although activities are happening spontaneously, you want to claim doership for them. But such a claim arises from your identity with the body-mind.

Having acquired spiritual knowledge, what are you going to do for the benefit of the world?

V: I will just *be*.

M: People who have a liking for social work want to do some good. They want to transform the quality of the intellect of other people so they live in harmony with each other.

V: The world is the expression of the truth and people should be helped to understand this.

M: If that is to happen, it will happen by itself. That which is changing continuously is the unreal. Change can be brought about only in the unreal. No change can be made in the real, the truth. In the world you can effect improvement in the concepts, but do not dare call the concepts the truth.

The truth can understand untruth; but can untruth understand truth? Just as you change garments, you change your concepts, and then you feel happy. The truth cannot be seen or perceived; but the truth can observe the untruth.

V: With concepts I shall not be happy. Is it correct?

M: You think that with concepts you can be happy. The happiness or bliss which reveals itself in the "no-concept" state cannot be perceived.

V: In life, there are moments of peace when we get a glimpse of the truth, and the faith developed as a result influences and guides our life.

M: These are only words, and words do not contain the truth. The truth does not need the help of words. Whatever you say is experience. But you are the experiencer, and without it also "you are." Experiences come and go, but the experiencer remains. You experience the world, but you are prior to the world. World is experiential, but "You," the Absolute, are non-experiential.

At present, the sense of "you-are-ness" is felt, but it is a temporary state; it will go. A hundred years ago—that is, prior to birth this "you-are-ness" was not associated with "You," the Absolute. This "you-are"-experience has come as a fever. How and why this fever has come, for this there is no explanation or reason.

V: In an instant, you came out of the sickness "you are." Is there any hope for me, too, to experience such a sublime moment?

M: Yes, provided you understand and assimilate this talk. Whatever is now, is the sense of being for all of us. First, one has to abide in it and finally, it is to be transcended.

V: This morning in meditation I felt I was not in the body-mind but only in the beingness.

M: That is the consciousness. It is the manifest state, in which there is no personality, no male or female. It is the knowledge "you are."

V: For some time, there was no sense of beingness also.

M: That was a state of stillness and only the consciousness was there.

V: Some say that the sense of "I am" is to the right side of the chest, about four fingers away from the center.

M: That depends upon individual experience. The location may vary according to the person. But do not understand or locate it with reference to the body.

[*An Indian seeker comes to Maharaj's place after roaming a lot in the neighborhood in search of the address.*]
M: Do you know this locality? Did you walk around a lot to find it?

V: Yes, Sir. I used to visit this area, a few years back, to meet a sage-like fakir.

M: Did he teach anything?

V: No. But he had certain powers. A few years ago, there was an explosion on a ship at anchor in the Bombay harbor. This fakir, who happened to be close by before the explosion, had a premonition. He shouted at the people around him and ordered them to rush out of the area immediately.
   Once he blessed me by patting me on the head, and I felt as if my *kundalini* energy rose upward.

M: That reminds me of another fakir of great attainments, by the name of Tikku-Baba. He lived in the Colaba district. Though I had not seen him personally, we used to have communication with each other through a messenger-fakir, who often used to visit my bidi[1] shop. Tikku-Baba had great powers for doing miracles. One day the messenger-fakir had gone to see Tikku-Baba late one night. To his consternation, he found Tikku-Baba's body dismembered and his limbs stacked together. Fearing that it might well be a case of murder, he ran away from the place where the fakir lived. Out of curiosity, he returned the next morning and to his great surprise found Tikku-Baba hale and hearty.

One day the messenger arrived at my shop with a message from Tikku-Baba that I should come and meet him at the earliest moment because his end was near. It was further conveyed that before he was to leave the body, he would like to transfer all his powers to me. In response I offered my thanks and told the messenger, "Please tell Tikku-Baba that the bargain is struck only once." By this I meant that a true disciple accepts a guru only for once and remains devoted to him and that he does not run after other gurus. When this message was received by Tikku-Baba, he remarked "Oh, he has reached the destination and is beyond any needs."

October 22nd 1980

---

1 Type of cheap Indian cigarette.

20.

HOLD ON TO YOUR
SENSE OF BEING

MAHARAJ: The universal consciousness is all-pervading, and it does not suffer any loss or gain as a result of interaction in the five-elemental play. However, in this process of interaction it manifests in a tangible way. [*Maharaj takes up a metal flower vase and drops it on the floor, which results in a clanging sound.*] When one object came in touch with another, the sound which was latent became apparent. [*Maharaj picks up a towel and points out that fire is latent in the cloth.*] Fire manifests only when there is action on the towel (i.e., by applying a flame to it), and as a reaction fire manifests and the towel burns. The consciousness is there all the time. Life is there all the time, and life will manifest itself when there is a form. Consciousness goes into action (i.e., becomes manifest, perceptible), just as the sound takes place or the cloth catches fire.

And similar to the fact that there is no particular identity for the sound or the fire, so there is no identity for the consciousness. Out of ignorance, and identification with the body, you experience pleasure and pain even though consciousness is universal and just functions through the body. So many people have died, so many people are murdered, but consciousness has ever remained the same. It has not been diminished or aggrandized in any way—it has not suffered at all. [*Maharaj again bangs the vase, and points out that the sound just happens.*] There is no pain or pleasure for the sound. It just manifests, so also the consciousness; it has no pain or pleasure. There is no loss or gain to the five elements. All these calamities that man experiences will not give pleasure or pain not only to the five elements, but also to the various qualities (*gunas*) perceived by the senses. The five qualities are: touch, form, smell, taste, and sound. Now, what is the significance of that "you" for you? Do not get involved in your wants. Where are you proceeding to? Think on these lines: the five elements are playing; and as a result of their interplay forms are created, and these are equipped with five senses. From the five-elemental objects—namely, vegetation and food—the form takes shape. Now, through this form, the consciousness manifests again the qualities (*gunas*) of the five elements. Ponder over this, and find out: What are you? and Where are you proceeding towards?

All along, thousands of wars have been fought. Now what has been the effect of all that on the five elements? These five elements are perceived by the five body senses. Because of the derailment of the five elements from the Highest, this *guna*—the consciousness—has emerged.

Suppose somebody is murdered, actually what did happen? The indwelling consciousness in the body that was murdered went into oblivion and functioning of the five senses came to a halt. Millions of people are killed and gone; did their five senses and their consciousness come to you, raising any disputes? With a body, five senses of perception and five limbs of action[1] are provided. With age, this body deteriorates and the senses and limbs no longer operate as effectively. Thus, with the gradual failure of the senses and limbs due to "ageing," the *guna* that is consciousness is also dwindling (that is, its manifestation, as such, weakens). In all these

---

1 In Hindu philosophy, the body's five limbs or organs of action are: tongue, feet, hands, and the organs of evacuation and procreation.

functions of the body, senses, limbs and consciousness, where do "you" fit in as such? And where do you proceed to? The various processes and events are due to the food body and *prana*; where is your position therein?

VISITOR: Is consciousness independent of body; that is, unaffected by it?

M: How can it be so? It is the outcome of the food-essence body and is called *sattva-guna*. Similarly, a child is also the essence of its parents' bodies. If a child is deformed, it is because of some inadequacy in the quality of the material food body.

The worldly activities, and also the spiritual ones carried out with the mind, are mere amusements in the state of ignorance. They began when the sense of being started to function with the cycle of waking and sleep.

If a person thinks that by practicing spirituality something can be gained, I would like to know the design and identity of such a one. Spiritual seekers, instead of inquiring into their very nature which is their consciousness, delve into spiritual books for knowledge.

V: Should we give up all the concepts and ideas collected thus far?

M: Do nothing of the sort. Just hold on to your sense of being so long as you know "you are," be only in that state. Do not worry about its going away.

V: Should we commit to memory the sense of being? But that would mean effort.

M: Where is the question of effort on your part? The consciousness spontaneously came into being. Consciousness itself is of the attention. Be there, do not try to alter or modify anything. Whatever "is," is there and that is the love of the self, *atma-prem*. If you can derive satisfaction by reading and following traditional, so-called spiritual paths and disciplines, by all means do it.

V: But Maharaj says we have to reach a destination.

M: Where is the question of proceeding to a destination and "who" is there to proceed? [*Maharaj bangs a piece of metal.*] Take this sound, where does it go? A *jnani* is totally away from all concepts. At that point there is nothing.

V: Yesterday, you spoke about guru and *sat-gurucharan*—the feet of the *sat-guru*.

M: Yes, I did. *Sat-gurucharan* means the spontaneous appearance of consciousness when you know "you are." Everything dwells in this knowledge "you are," and it is limitless and all-prevailing. This state represents the sacred feet of *sat-guru*.

V: I mean no offense at all when I ask a silly question. Why are there so many photographs on these walls? I feel this goes contrary to your teaching.

M: They are the relics of the period of ignorance. To dispel the ignorance such aids are necessary. When the purpose is served, they are no longer required. This body which I use is also an outcome of the ignorant stage, but it is still in use though I have transcended the stage of ignorance. So let the photographs remain to decorate the walls; there is no harm in that. Instead of changing things on the outside, why not bring about a change within by removing your wrong identities?

You talk as if you have wisdom, but what knowledge have you actually? Your present capital is the cycle of waking, deep sleep, and knowledge "I am." What else have you got? This cycle has appeared by itself without your asking; all else you have learned and acquired later. Anybody who comes here is like an ignorant child, in spite of whatever so-called knowledge he has gained from outside.

November 13th 1980

21.

RETURN TO THE STATE
BEFORE BIRTH

MAHARAJ: I once felt a sense of individuality, but I do not now have that individuality. The sense of individuality has transformed itself into the universal manifest state.

VISITOR: Did it happen just like that?

M: The moment the name of the disease emerged, the feeling of being an individual arose. Now the sense of individuality is gone and only the feeling of universal consciousness remains.

The individuality is gone, together with the identity of body form. The body is not my design, nor am I male or female. Everything happens spontaneously. Who sees that the day has dawned and the sun shines? Could the knowledge of the day be the individual's? The moment one wakes up, the "I-am-ness" arises, which means the sense of being only; later also the sense of body is there. This sense of beingness is all-pervading, and it has no name and no form—it is existence itself.

V: When the body suffers, what actually happens? What is the relationship between the Unmanifest and the body, or between the actual and the illusory appearances in the world?

M: They are intimately related. The culture and sentiment of every atom is different, so also every individual is different in this world.

There are varieties of expressions in atoms and sub-atoms.

V: Is the truth manifest or unmanifest? If the truth manifests through the body, then all the diseases of the body are in the Unmanifest.

M: When the Unmanifest manifests, it is called *saguna-brahman*. This *brahman* principle is ample, plenty and manifest and comprises the five elements, three *gunas* and *prakriti-purush*; it is this that recognizes the sun and the space and is more pervasive and subtler than space even.

V: What is all this play about? In this manifest universe, which is the outcome of the Unmanifest, a body suffers from sickness—the body of Maharaj. As a result, we also suffer, after witnessing the sickness. Why all this nuisance?

M: If your "I-am-ness" is not, who would observe the rising of the sun?

V: Although you have explained it thousands of times, I still have not understood.

M: "Who" and "what," as such at the highest level, are Nothing; whatever *is*, is very clear and obvious. But such a simple fact has turned into a riddle, because that principle has identified itself wrongly with a form, and then takes pride in that identification. It has accepted body as its identity.

V: But why should this happen to you through whose body the Unmanifest manifests itself?

M: In order to have a reply to this question, you will have to retreat into yourself.

Out of this atomic touch, this speck of consciousness, all this magnificent universe has materialized. How and what would you reply to this question: Did it create itself or did it arrange for the creation? Your replies will be mere conjecture and guesswork. What evidence have you that you have births and deaths? What proof have you about rebirth?

V: You mean to say that we should remain at the point of emergence of consciousness? Shall we then understand this?

M: Yes, I have been telling people exactly that.

V: Then you mean to say that unless I stop at the rising of consciousness, I shall not understand this play of the Unmanifest, manifest, body suffering etc., and that all my talking is actually only blabbering and therefore a mere nuisance.

M: Yes, it is just entertainment to pass the time.

V: That means when we visit and sit near you, in fact it bothers you.

M: I am not bothered even by the five elements, which are my creations. So how can you be a nuisance to me? If I identify myself with the body, then I will necessarily have to undergo all the botherations and sufferings that go with it.

V: May I ask you another question? You have consciousness which has reached a certain high level. Could it have a beneficial effect on us by your mere presence without any talk?

M: Not only you, but even germs, ants, worms and so on, are the beneficiaries.

V: That means your influence is continuously working on us, including on the smallest?

M: For the sake of talking it is all right, but in actuality no one affects anyone. At the moment of its sprouting, did my birth principle have any intelligence? This birth principle, which is the child principle, grows spontaneously, develops mind and intellect and may in due course become a Mahatma—a great sage even—but the root of that sage is the sprouting of the child principle only. Is it not so? Now you are collecting a lot of knowledge in the name of spirituality, but that is only entertainment.

V: How can a child principle attain the status of a *jnani* or sage?

M: To understand this, stay there at the point of sprouting (*ankura*), you be the *ankura* (*omkara*). [Om *is the beginning of words and Maharaj directs the visitor to be in a state prior to the formation of words in his mind.*]

V: That is all right and I decide to remain in that *omkara* state. Then what about the violence which goes on outside— in Iran, America, the USSR etc.? Is there no connection or have I to sit passively in the *omkara* state?

M: Both are intimately connected.

V: But to escape from violence, suffering, exploitation . . .

M: All your talk is in defence of your individuality. As a matter of fact, you are to be accused of responsibility for all that is happening. Except you, who could be the accused? To say all that, who is there but you, your sense of "I-am-ness"? To state "anything is," someone must be there in the first place.

In your beingness, millions of sins are committed and

now you want to elude responsibility by clinging to, and hiding within, an individuality. All these happenings are your creations only.

V: But you are also all that, in your beingness.

M: Totally everything is in my beingness, including yourself. But no authority whatsoever is given either to me or to you to set things right.

V: To set matters right, can the *omkara* be of any use?

M: *Omkara* is useful for everything; and all is *omkara*, including suffering. How else could there be pleasure and pain without the realm of *omkara*? Whatever sprouted is termed as birth, and with birth beingness wrongly identifies itself as a personality—resulting in pleasure and pain.

V: With *omkara*, how can the *ankura* (sprouting) be stopped?

M: In the same way that it sprouted.

V: Can the *omkara* arrest the sprouting (*ankura*) or is the *ankura* a play of the *omkara*?

M: *Omkara* and *ankura* are both experiential states. Could they be separate? What can there be without *omkara*?

V: I want to know if there is a process which can arrest *ankura*—sprouting? Say, by reciting the sacred mantra *omkara*; or should we passively watch all the happenings?

M: Every mantra has a purpose; there cannot be any mantra without a purpose.

V: Then by reciting a mantra everything will be re-created?

M: Yes.

V: Then why should we recite a mantra at all?

M: But this mantra is without any language, without any words. Go to the root, see the actuality before you die, abide in your true nature. But instead, you are busy pampering your body which you consider as your identity. People are devotional to God only in order to acquire things worldly.

V: That means our devotion to God is equal to going into the marketplace for a purchase.

M: This is the way that human life goes on. The normal motive force is gain for all one's actions.

V: So long as one worships God with the aim of gain, the worship will not be effective; isn't that so?

M: The primary motive is the "love-to-be," to keep oneself alive.

V: When the "love-to-be" is lost, what happens?

M: Who is there to reply?
   When the "love-to-be" has subsided, who is there to say that it has subsided? Is it possible to experience *shakti* (energy potential), *ananda* (bliss) and *sat-chid-ananda* (being-consciousness-bliss)? Or is there nothing of the sort?

V: We have been told about *sat-chit* and *ananda* all along. If they are real, should we not proceed towards them? And if they do not exist as such, why should we strive at all for them?

M: Our source, the root, is our sense of beingness, or the child principle. Did it engage in any activity consciously? Did it have any intelligence at all, at that stage? What else is there, except this primary child principle?

V: Let someone ask questions now.

M: How can they ask real questions? They will pose questions after holding on to some identity, and such identities are built up after reading or listening to somebody. All this is informational knowledge collected externally, and it is not the spontaneous knowledge, the true knowledge. Who has the knowledge that "one is" and what is that "one is"? What is this principle of Shiva? In Marathi, *shiv* means "a touch." Show me the touch of beingness. Thoroughly observe and investigate: How did this principle, the touch of beingness, happen to be? The entire cosmic expression is the proliferation of the touch of beingness. This principle comprises the five elements, three *gunas* and *prakriti-purush*.

V: All this magnificent creation is out of *omkara*, the touch of beingness. Is it an energy, a power, or merely a notion?

M: Whatever words, titles, or ideas occur to you, are all right for the purpose.

V: To this principle, titles such as Jagadamba—mother of the universe—Mahishasura Mardini—destroyer of the demon Mahisha etc. are given.

M: What do you mean by Jagadamba? The principle which recognizes the daybreak, the waking state, is that Jagadamba?

V: But is this principle an energy or only a concept, or an illusion?

M: Has it intelligence?

V: Is it a sort of intelligence?

M: You may presume it to be so.

V: What I want to know is this: This manifestation which has come out of me, am I a part of it or am I apart from it?

M: You are not apart from it. It is your light only.

V: Time and again is has been proclaimed through various religions, *tantras*, *puranas* etc. that it is an energy potential, it is *ananda*, it is *shakti*, it is charged with love etc. These are our deep-rooted impressions, and once we give them up, once we surrender them, what are we to do?

M: Where is the need to surrender them?

V: You have given me two levels: at one level I see this relationship between my manifestation and Me, and the other level is the sprouting or rising of the sense of "I-am-ness." What am I to do?

M: If you are interested in levels, there are millions of them and you may start counting. But that principle cannot be objectified as a sample for the purpose of counting. What are you? What do you feel you are, what is your specimen?

What is the point in your running about here and there for social work etc. . . .

In this objective world is there anything permanent? You are trying to do so many things, such as social services, to make people happy.

You shave today, and tomorrow again you have to shave as your beard grows, and so on. Similarly, you make people happy today, and tomorrow they are unhappy, and again you proceed to make them happy, and so the cycle goes on, and you are caught in it. Initially, when I wanted to pursue spirituality, I gave up *prapancha*, the worldly life. Later I understood the meaning of spirituality and came to the conclusion that it is as discardable as used dishwater. Therefore, at present, I am in no way concerned with spirituality, since I have transcended it. I cannot discuss the topic in this manner before the general public. They would throw stones at me. What are you? What is your identity? Have you seen yourself correctly? Can you take photographs of your true identity bereft of body-mind? With this type of talk, will you care to see me again?

V: Maharaj, after such visits when I had the great privilege of associating with you, this personage known as Nisargadatta Maharaj, I have a feeling of having been given a certain push in my spiritual pursuit. Maybe this feeling, which persists for three, four months after such visits, is a sort of bewildering state of exultation. It gives an assurance that one can stop at the point of *ankura*—the "sprouting of I-am-ness." This feeling itself is an indication of wisdom and intuitive apperception.

In the past three or four years when I visited you, I went back with these impressions and I used to get some peace—a sort of quietude.

M: Yes, but that is the mere subsidence of your mental turbulence. Beyond this, it is nothing.

V: But Maharaj, is it bad? We get the feeling of quietude and well-being after the visits. Why do you denounce it?

M: It is only a temporary state; after some time it will disappear. With birth, three states—deep sleep, waking and knowingness—function. What you experienced is in the domain of knowingness, a time-bound state. Prior to birth, is there any need for anything?

November 20th 1980

GLOSSARY

acharya — great preceptor, a widely respected teacher, a
spiritual master

advaita — non–duality

aham–bhava — the "I–am" sense

aham–kara — literally "I–maker"; the "I–am" or ego; the
sense of doership, ownership, etc.

ajanma — "without birth," uncreated, beginningless;
the Unborn

alak — non–attention

amrita — nectar, ambrosia

ananda — bliss, transcendent joy

ananda mayi — consisting of bliss, filled with bliss

Ananda Mayi Ma — "Bliss–filled Mother," name of a highly
regarded female saint, a contemporary of Maharaj

ankura — sprout, the sprouting (of "I–am–ness")

arati — ritual in which a lamp with an open flame is waved
before a sacred image or picture; in Marathi "special
need," love of each creature for self

asanas — postures, like those in yoga

atma, atman — Self; the true, spiritual Self, as opposed to
the empirical self, the body–mind

atma–jnana — Self–knowledge, direct realization of the
atman

atma–prem — self–love, love of the empirical self or love of
the *atman*, the higher Self

atma–sutra — the "thread of the Self," the Universal Self
that runs through and supports the cosmos

atma–yoga — the discipline or way of Self–knowledge; the
practice that leads to knowledge of the *atman*

avatar — divine incarnation

balkrishna — literally "child Krishna," "boy Krishna," a
reference to the playful childhood of the *avatar* Krishna; in

Maharaj's usage, the "child–consciousness," the "I–am–ness" feeling before the formation of the mind

Bhagavan Vasudeva — literally "Lord Krishna"; in Maharaj's usage here, the God who gives the "I–am–ness" fragrance

bhajans — devotional songs, in which the Divine Name is chanted, an important feature of *bhakti–yoga*

bhakti — devotion, love of God

bhakti–yoga — the path of loving devotion to God, in which God is approaching in an attitude of loving surrender

bija — seed, source

bodhisattva — in Buddhism, an enlightened being who remains in the world to help others attain enlightenment

Brahman — the Absolute Reality

Brahma–sutra — the "thread of Brahman," Brahman as that which runs through and supports the world

brihaspati — literally "Lord of the immense magnitude," in Hindu lore, the name of the *guru* of the gods; sometimes used by Maharaj to designate the human species

charan–amrita — nectar of the Lord's feet, the perfumed "holy water" with which the feet of an image of a deity have been washed; considered especially sacred

chit — consciousness, Universal Consciousness, the Self

dhyana–yoga — the path of meditation, a meditative approach towards spirituality

diksha — initiation

ganesha — realization of the "I–am–ness" state; the state prior to *para* in the formation of language; also, the name of a deity

guru–bhakti — devotion to the spiritual preceptor

hatha–yoga — a Hindu system of physical culture, designed to prepare the body for long periods of meditation

hatha–yogin — a practitioner of *hatha–yoga*

hiranyagarbha — literally, "Golden Embryo"; consciousness
humkara — the sound "hum," the humming sound (of beingness) heard in meditation

Ishwara — the Lord, God
Ishwara-bhakti — devotion to God

Jagadamba — Mother of the Universe
japa — the reciting of holy names of God; in Marathi "to guard, protect"
jnana — knowledge, more particularly, spiritual knowledge
jnana-yoga — the yoga of knowledge
jnani — literally "possessed of knowledge," "knower"; a realized sage

karma — activity, movement; the moral consequences of one's actions that, returning to the doer, create future experiences, good or bad
kundalini — the universal spiritual energy (*shakti*) that lies dormant at the base of the spine and is activated through spiritual practice
kundalini-yoga — the yoga of *kundalini*, a practice that seeks spiritual progress and power by awakening the *kundalini* energy

madhyama — the middle stage of the manifestation of speech and consciousness, between *pashyanti* and *vaikhari*, in which the tangible formation of speech begins
maha-tattva — literally "Great Principle"; consciousness
maha-vakya — literally "great statement"; a saying from the *Upanishads* expressing the truth of Brahman, the Supreme Reality

maha-yoga — literally "the Great Union"; use by Maharaj to designate the borderline of beingness and non-beingness
mahatma — Great Soul

Maheshwara — "Supreme Lord," God

Mahishasura Mardini — Destroyer of the demon Mahishasura, a name of Durga (considered an aspect of Kali, the Divine Mother)

Mahisha — buffalo; the name of a demon, Mahishasura, who appeared as a great buffalo

manojaya — victory over the mind

mantra — a sacred word or verbal formula that has the potency to elevate and purify the mind by connecting it with the Divine; a fixed series of sacred words

Marathi — the language spoken in Bombay and Maharashtra State, where Maharaj lived

maya — the cosmic illusion, more particularly the primordial illusion of identification with the body; the dynamic principle of manifestation that projects the cosmic illusion and conceals the transcendent unity.

moola — a root (as of a tree), the basis, foundation; in Marathi, a child

moolamaya —the root or foundational illusion; the borderline between being and "non–being"

nama–japa — repetition of a holy Name of God

namasmarana — recitation of a holy Name of God

Navanath Sampradaya — traditional order of the Nine Gurus (see *I Am That*, first American edition, p. 539)

neti–neti — "not this, not that," an Upanishadic saying whose purport is that the supreme Brahman is beyond any attribute or quality.

nirguna — the "attributeless," unconditioned, non–qualitative state; the Absolute Brahman, "non–beingness"

niroopa — message, representation

niroopana — demonstration, a spiritual talk or discourse affording proof

nirvana — state of non–identity or total transcendence of ego; the loss of the sense of "I–am–ness"; the *Parabrahman*

nirvishaya — without object, the state in which there is no

object of perception and hence, no subject; state of
"non–beingness"

niryana — state prevailing upon extinguishing of the sense of
"I–am–ness"

nishkama Parabrahman — the desireless (*nishkama*) state of
the supreme Absolute (*Parabrahman*)

Om (or *Aum*) — sacred sound, the primordial sound that
embodies the essential Reality, manifest and unmanifest

Omkar(a) — the sound "Om" (see above); state prior to
the formation of words

pancha–pranas — five–fold vital breath

para — the Supreme; the source of speech; the Absolute

Parabrahman — the supreme state of the Absolute; the state
before space–time, before manifestation; the Unborn
eternal principle, the state "higher" than "I am" or
beingness which is transitory

parabdhi — the "great ocean"; the ocean of life; time; death

Paramatman — the Supreme Self, the eternal Absolute state

parama–vishranti — supreme repose, the highest state of
dwelling in the Absolute

Parameshwara — the "Supreme Lord," name of Shiva;
the Absolute

para–shakti — the Supreme Energy; as *para*, the supreme
state of speech

para–vani — Supreme Speech, the transcendent state of
speech, same as *para*, *para–shakti*

pashyanti — the incipient stage of the manifestation
of speech

poornabrahman — the Infinite Brahman

prakriti–purush(a) — "Matter and Spirit," the dual
female–male principle creating the five elements and
three *gunas*

prakriti–purusha shakti — the "energy of matter and spirit";
in Maharaj's usage, beingness

prana — the vital breath, life energy

pranava — Om, the primordial sound

prapancha — the manifest world, worldly life

prarabdha — destiny, the *karma* that determines the course
of this present life

prasada — blessed food that has been spiritualized by
offering to a deity or guru

puranas — sacred writings, Hindu scriptures recounting
sacred history and the stories of the deities

purusha — the principle of pure Spirit or consciousness,
symbolically male; the Awareness that witnesses the
cosmic display of *prakriti* or *maya*

purusha–prakriti — "Spirit and Matter," same as
prakriti–purusha

Purushottama — the highest *purusha*, the supreme Spirit; the
Absolute, the Eternal

rajas — energy, passion, dynamic quality; one of the
three *gunas*

rishis — seers, the sages of ancient times

saguna–brahman — Brahman "with attributes," the manifest,
conditioned aspect of Brahman, in Maharaj's usage the
sense of "I–am–ness", beingness

samadhi — literally "absorption"; the highest stage of yogic
meditation, often described as "trance–like"

samskaras — subliminal impressions registered in the
unconscious, created by experience in this and
previous lives

sangh — monastic order

sat–chid–ananda — Being–Consciousness–Bliss; in Vedanta
philosophy, the "essential definition" of the nature
of Brahman

sat–guru — true preceptor, genuine spiritual teacher

sat–gurucharan — the feet of the *sat–guru*

sattva — consciousness; also seed–beingness; clarity, purity, harmony; one of the three *gunas*

sattva-shakti — literally, the "energy of purity"; in Maharaj's usage, beingness

savishaya — literally, "with object"; the state in which subject and object are present; in Maharaj's usage, beingness

shakti — energy, power, spiritual energy

Sheshashayi — name of Vishnu as "He who lies on the coils of the cosmic serpent, Shesha"

shiv — in Marathi, a touch

shuddhavijnana — pure knowledge; pure "Superknowledge"

siddhapurushas — highly evolved souls

siddhis — "supernatural" powers

svadharma — the particular life course laid out for one, one's "own duty"

svarasa — the essence or "juice" of a thing, in Maharaj's usage, "sense of knowingness"

svarupananda — bliss of one's own nature (*svarupa*); the bliss of being

tamas — inertia, resistance, darkness, one of the three *gunas*; also the claiming of doership

tantra — a body of techniques of consciousness–elevation, including mantra and *yantra*; a text explaining such techniques

tapa — the practice of austerities

tat tvam asi — "Thou Art That," a famous Vedantic *mahavakya* (see above)

vachaspati — literally "Lord of Speech," a deity in Hindu mythology; in Maharaj's usage, a name for the animal kingdom, including human beings

vaikhari — the final state in the manifestation of speech, after *para*, *pashyanti*, and *madhyama*

vanaspati — literally, "Lord of the Forest," the vegetable kingdom *vasanas* — latent impressions that reside in the subconscious; innate tendencies

videhisthiti — the body–free state, unembodiedness

vishara–anti — Maharaj's etymology of *vishranti*, meaning final self–forgetting

vishranti — absolute rest, complete relaxation leading to total forgetfulness in meditation

vishva–sutra — the "thread of the Universe," that which runs through the universe, holding it together

vishvavishaya — the cosmos as object of perception, the universal manifestation

vishvayoga — unity with the cosmos

vritti — mental modification, a fluctuation of the mind

yantra — object for ritualistic worship, typically a mystic diagram

yogamaya — the power of manifestation, beingness, the manifest state

yogashakti — cosmic energy

yoga — literally "yoked" or "union," spiritual discipline or practice designed to purify one's mind and bring one closer to Self–realization

BIBLIOGRAPHY

Balsekar, Ramesh S. *Pointers from Nisargadatta*. Bombay,
   India: Chetana; Durham, N.C.: The Acorn Press, 1982.
Brent, Peter. *Godmen of India*. Harmondsworth, Middlesex,
   England: Penguin Books, 1972.
Nisargadatta, Maharaj. *I Am That: Talks with Sri
   Nisargadatta Maharaj*, Translated from the
   Marathi by Maurice Frydman, and edited by Sudhakar
   S. Dikshit. Bombay, India: Chetana; Durham, N.C.:
   The Acorn Press, 1994.
_____. *Consciousness and the Absolute*. Edited by Jean
   Dunn. Durham, N.C.: The Acorn Press, 1994.
_____. *Prior to Consciousness*. Edited by Jean Dunn.
   Durham, N.C.: The Acorn Press, second edition, 1990.
_____. *Seeds of Consciousness*. Edited by Jean Dunn.
   Durham, N.C.: The Acorn Press, second edition, 1990.
_____, *The Ultimate Medicine*. Edited by Robert Powell.
   San Diego: Blue Dove Press, 2001
_____, *The Experience of Nothingness*. Edited by Robert
Powell. San Diego: Blue Dove Press, 2001
Powell, Robert. *The Blissful Life*. Durham, N.C.: The
   Acorn Press, 1984.
_____. *The Wisdom of Sri Nisargadatta Maharaj*.
   San Diego: Blue Dove Press, 1995
Sri Nisargadatta Maharaj Presentation Volume: 1980.
   Bombay, India: Sri Nisargadatta Adhyatma Kendra,
1981.

Offerings from
The Robert Powell
Advaita Library

From Blue Dove Press:

Beyond Religion
Meditations on Our True Nature
by Robert Powell, Ph.D.
Softcover   221 pp. $15.95   ISBN: 1-884997-31-7

In this collection of selected essays, reflections, and public talks, Dr. Robert Powell— one of the foremost contemporary writers of *Advaita* philosophy—addresses such topics as Consciousness, Meditation, Existence, World Peace, and the Arrival of the Third Millennium, and addresses their relation to spiritual awakening and "human consciousness transformation".

Excerpt from the book:
What is the need for religion, for a so-called spiritual orientation in life, at all? If living is a natural function, like breathing, then why interfere? Why can we not continue in our naturally more or less hedonistic way? This would be true if our minds were still functioning in their natural ways, free of complexity, flowing with life. This assumption, as we all know, is no longer valid—if it ever was. Our minds are heavily conditioned, fragmented and deep in contradiction. This conflict in the mind leads inevitably to conflict in society, and thus to chaos. So even if we opted for a simple hedonistic way of life, sooner or later this would be compromised by the ways of the mind.
        True religion or spirituality is nothing other than the reversal of this whole process of chaos, conflict, to a state of simplicity, naturalness, and therefore order...

Dialogues on Reality
An Exploration into the Nature of Our Ultimate Identity
by Robert Powell, Ph.D.

Softcover   236 pp. $14   ISBN: 1-884997-16-3

"Dr. Powell is one of the best known Western writers on Advaita *philosophy. He comments elegantly on the insights of Krishnamurti and Sri Nisargadatta Maharaj, and explains his own insights on the nature of the unified state. You will find great gems in his books. "*— **Deepak Chopra**
Author of *Ageless Body, Timeless Mind* and *Quantum Healing*

Dr. Powell is widely recognized as one of the most inspired writers on the subject of *Advaita*, the teaching of non-duality. He takes us on a journey beyond the realm of the ego, beyond the subject and object, good and bad, high and low, to the ground on which the manifest universe rests. This is where the mind and intellect cannot reach and which is beyond words. Yet in this book, Dr. Powell does a masterful job clearly indicating the path to where we have ever been.

Excerpt from the book:
"You see, the psychologist starts from the wrong basis. His methodology is founded upon the assumption that there really is a 'person,' an ego, that can be free, whereas what we are trying to point out is that the ego itself, which comprises both the conscious and the unconscious, is totally a composite of falseness and the source of all trouble; it alone destroys freedom and nothing else does...You see that you are not within the world, you are not a small entity in a very large world but the opposite is the case...The whole world of phenomena, entities, creatures, is within my consciousness. And that consciousness has no boundaries, no divisions; it is infinity itself." — **Robert Powell**

Discovering the Realm Beyond Appearance

Pointers to the Inexpressible

by Robert Powell, Ph.D

Softcover   200 pp. $14.00   ISBN: 1-884997-17-1

"Drawing upon a rich and diverse stream of religious traditions from Hinduism to Zen Buddhism, Powell argues that the path to spiritual peace and happiness comes through a transformation to the advaitic mode of life....Powell ranges over such topics as death, reincarnation, religious beliefs, morality and spirituality. In fluid and accessible prose, Powell opens the doors to self-awareness through meditation and other advaitic teachings. " — **Publishers Weekly**

"Dr. Powell is one of the best known Western writers on Advaita *philosophy.... All those seeking higher levels of awareness will find powerful tools in* Discovering the Realm Beyond Appearance. *"*— **Deepak Chopra**
Author of *The Seven Spiritual Laws of Success*

Excerpt from the book:

"The meaning of your existence is primarily to realize your true nature, that you are not just an 'individual,' so that your life may stand in service of the world as a whole and make it a little less miserable. All else is mere entertainment, without ultimate meaning....

"But once you have realized your true nature, when individuality has been seen for the illusion it is and so has been transcended once and for all, there is only the Totality. Now where could the Totality go? It is at once everything, completely fulfilled—it is fulfillment itself. Therefore, the question of meaning cannot apply for one, or more accurately, for That which has realized itself. We can only talk of 'meaning' when there is intentionality, direction, a movement from here to there, from incomplete to complete, applying to a fragment, the false image of an 'entity.' It could not possibly apply to that which by definition is Everything, Complete and Perfect in Itself."

The Ultimate Medicine
As Prescribed by Sri Nisargadatta Maharaj
Edited by Robert Powell, Ph.D.
Softcover   240 pp. $14.95   ISBN: 1-884997-09-0

"...Nisargadatta, like all the great sages of old India, elucidates the nature of the Ultimate Reality clearly and simply. He makes the highest Self-realization a matter of common understanding so that any sincere seeker can grasp the essence of it."
— **David Frawley, O.M.D.**, author of *Beyond the Mind,* and *Ayurvedic Healing*

"...Sri Nisargadatta Maharaj will be increasingly recognized as a wholly admirable star in the spiritual firmament of our age."
— **Peter V. Madill, M.D.**

Sri Nisargadatta Maharaj (1897-1981), one of the most important spiritual preceptors of the twentieth century, lived and taught in a small apartment in the slums of Bombay, India. A realized master of the Tantric Nath lineage, Maharaj had a wife and four children. For many years he supported his family by selling inexpensive goods in a small booth on the streets outside his tenement. His life was a telling parable of the absolute nonduality of Being.

The simple words of this extraordinary teacher are designed to jolt us into awareness of our original nature. His style is abrupt, provocative and immensely profound— wasting little time with nonessentials and cutting directly to the core.

A steady stream of Indians and Westerners came to sit at the feet of Maharaj in the small loft where he received visitors. There, in the tradition of Ramana Maharshi, he shared the highest Truth of nonduality in his own unique way, from the depths of his own realization.

In *The Ultimate Medicine*, Nisargadatta provides advanced instructions for serious spiritual aspirants.

The Experience of Nothingness
Sri Nisargadatta Maharaj's Talks on Realizing the Infinite
Edited by Robert Powell, Ph.D.
Softcover   183 pp. $14.95   ISBN: 1-884997-14-7

"Sri Nisargadatta Maharaj hardly needs an introduction any longer to lovers of the highest wisdom. Known as a maverick Hindu sage, Nisargadatta is now generally acknowledged to rank with the great masters of advaita teachings, such as Sri Ramana Maharshi...,Sri Atmananda...,and the more recently known disciple of the Maharshi, Poonjaji..."— **Robert Powell**

In this final volume of the Nisargadatta Maharaj trilogy published by Blue Dove Press, the ever-trenchant Nisargadatta uses Socratic dialogue, wry humor, and his incisive intellect to cut through the play of consciousness which constitutes illusion: this is his only goal. He can relentlessly pursue a logical argument to its very end clearly demonstrating that logic and spirituality do not necessarily stand in opposition to one another.

Nisargadatta uses every device in his command to great effect, turning his visitors' questions back on themselves, making them laugh at the very concept of "concepts" and ultimately revealing that the emperor "mind" indeed has no clothes.

Excerpt from the book:
"Everything that is there, it is fullness and it is nothingness. So long as I do not have that 'I-am-ness,' I no longer have the concept that I am an individual. Then my individuality has merged into this everythingness or nothingness and everything is all right."— **Sri Nisargadatta Maharaj**

Path Without Form
A Journey into the Realm Beyond Thought
by Robert Powell, Ph.D

Softcover   242 pp. $14.95   ISBN: 1-884997-21-X

*".... 'adventures in self-exploration'— but with a twist....
Readers versed in Hindu thought will most likely be intrigued by
the way Powell spins out its implications for authentic
living...."*— **Library Journal**

"This book can serve as a primer for spiritual seekers."
        — **Georg Feuerstein**
        Author of *Yoga: The Technology of Ecstasy*

"Dr. Powell is one of the best known Western writers on
Advaita *philosophy.... You will find great gems in his books."*
        — **Deepak Chopra**
        Author of *The Seven Spiritual Laws of Success*

"Recommended." — **American Library Journal**

Excerpt from the book:
        "The ultimate teaching is the seeing of the entire world
in not even a grain of sand, but a single point—and a point that
is dimensionless. That mystical 'point' then serves as the entry
into an entirely new dimension—the world of the truly
spiritual....However, for the individual embracing this ultimate
teaching, the vision of the non-duality of reality does not mean
that he has arrived. On the contrary, it is a mere beginning and
the understanding has to be tested in life's experience, so that
each moment is a new reality. This process of learning, from
moment to moment, is a never-ending movement. But without
that vision of the wholeness of things, nothing is of avail; we
cannot travel on the spiritual path...."
        —Robert Powell

Lights of Grace
Catalog
from
The Blue Dove Foundation

The Blue Dove Foundation is a non-profit, tax-exempt organization and not affiliated with any particular path, tradition, or religion. Our mission is to deepen the spiritual life of all by making available works on the lives, messages, and examples of saints and sages of all religions and traditions, as well as other spiritual titles that provide tools for inner growth.

The Blue Dove Foundation supports the publication of inspirational books and tapes from Blue Dove Press. The foundation also distributes important spiritual works of other publishers, including hundreds of titles from India, through our web site and *Lights of Grace* catalog.

From Saint Teresa of Avila, to Sri Ramana Maharshi, to Milarepa, the Tibetan yogi—from *The Koran*, to *The Zohar*, to *The Mahabharata*—we have assembled an inspired collection of spiritual works at its most diverse and best.

For a free Catalog contact:

The Blue Dove Foundation
4204 Sorrento Valley Blvd. Suite K
San Diego, CA 92121
Phone: (858)623-3330 FAX: (858)623-3325
Orders: (800)691-1008
e-mail: bdp@bluedove.org
Web site: www.bluedove.org